Gran's Cottage

Copyright © 2002 Susan
13435 N.E. Whitaker W
PH(503)254-9100 Fax (503)252-9508
PRINTED IN THE USA
e-mail: scheewepub@aol.com
web site: http://www.painting-books.com

We have lived in the same little house for 35 years. It is a snug cozy little "Cottage" filled with Memories, Love, laughter and lots of painted goodies. Welcome to my Cottage and I hope you have a great time painting my pieces.

Paige, Caroline and Macroni spend lots of time with me out in my workroom with all the wood, paint, brushes and great stuff.

Ros Stallcup
1436 Lakeview Drive
Virginia Beach, Va. 23455
757-464-4974 Fax 757-464-4185
E-mail: Stalcop@aol.com
Web site: www.gransgarden.com

All rights reserved under the Pan American International Copyright conventions. No part of this publication may be reproduced or utilized in any form or by any mechanical or electronic means, including photocopying, photographing, computer scanning or any information storage and retrieval system without permission from the publisher.

The information in this book is presented in good faith: however, no warranty is given nor are results guaranteed. Susan Scheewe Publications Inc. disclaims any liability for untoward results. Patterns may only be hand traced for personal use or teaching only. Not for commercial reproduction or mass marketing such as the gift industry. The designs in this book are protected by copyright; however, you may make the designs for your personal use or to sell in local craft markets.

Sources

Stan Brown's Arts and Craft
13435 N E Whitaker Way
Portland, OR 97230
P 800-547-5531
F 503-252-9508
www.stanbrownartsandcrafts.com

Susan Scheewe Publications
13435 N E Whitaker Way
Portland, OR 97230
P 503-254-9100
F 503-252-9508
www.painting-books.com

Lavender Cat
1109 RT 206
Mountain View Plaza
Belle Mead, NJ 08502
P 908-359-4490

Russ Hayden
1004 McKinley Ave
Chesapeake, VA 23324
P 757-406-2295

Stephs' Folk Art Studio
2435 Old Philadelphia Pike
Smoketown, PA 17576
P 717-299-4973

Park Shop
164 Buffalo St
Hamburg, NY 14075
P 716-648-2577

Cabin Crafters
1225 West Street
Nevada, Iowa
P 800-669-3920
F 515-382-3016

Fergie's Tole Shop Inc
8730 49th Street North
Suite 4
Pinellas Park, FL33782
P 727-545-3713

Waynes's Woodenware
1913 CTH II
Nenah WI 54956
P 800-840-1497
e-mail waynesvbe.com

Country Crafts
272 Larkfield Rd
E. Northport NY 11731
P 631-757-8659

Taylors Arts and Crafts
800 Carbon City Rd.
Morganton, NC 28655
P 828-584-4771

Country Crafts
272 Larkfield Rd
E. Northport, NY 11731
P 613-757-8659

Supplies

All painting supplies can be purchased at your local art and craft stores. Some may be found in hardware stores or paint and wallpaper stores. Whenever possible I have listed source information.

Paints

I have used DecoArt Americana Acrylic paints. Colors are listed in each project and always refer to the color pictures. Similar colors will work. It doesn't have to be exactly the same shade. Make your own color charts. Put your color samples alphabetically in an inexpensive address book. Take your book with you to classes where paints are supplied and add those colors too.

Brushes

Suzie's Foliage Brush is a natural bristle brush cut on an angle. All other brushes are soft synthetic hair.

Flats Shaders - Nos. 4, 6, 10, & 16
Rounds - Nos. 2 & 5
Liner - No. 0
Angular Shaders - 3/8", 1/2" & 3/4" (Scheewe Angular Shader, S8008 Martin/F. Weber)
Filberts (Cat's Tongue) - Nos. 2, 4, 8, & 12
Oval Wash Brush - 1/2" & 3/4"
Suzie's Foliage Brush - 1/2" & 3/4" (Scheewe Foliage Angular, S8037 Martin/F. Weber)
Lettering Brush - 1/8" # 580 Winsor Newton
Fan Brush 2/0 (#916 Stan Brown's Arts & Crafts) or 10/0 Loew Cornel'

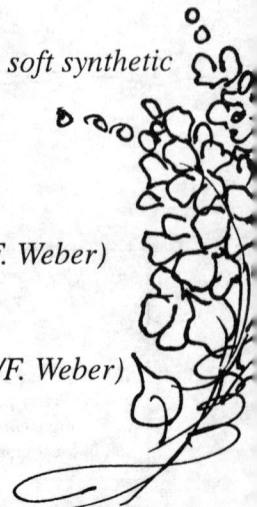

Supplies continued
General Supplies

- Water Container
- Masking Tape (3M)
- Acrylic Palette Paper with Deli-Wrap
- Brown Pigma Pens (.01)
- Black Pigma Pens (.01)
- Paper Towels
- Stylus or a Red Ink Ballpoint Pen
- Tracing Paper
- Write-on Transparency Film (for practice)

- Scheewe Gesso
- Crayola ChalkBoard Paint
- J.W. Right Step Waterbase Varnish
- J.W. White Lightening
- J.W. First Step Wood Sealer
- J.W. Wood Filler
- Plastic T-square
- Sandpaper
- Graphite Paper - White and Gray

Lettering

I do my lettering on my computer. There are loads of great fonts to pick from. Just type in, enlarge under page set up and print. Trim your print out and transfer.

Measure and find the center of your board. Draw a light pencil line through the center. Measure where you want the bottom of your letters to be and draw a straight line with a ruler or T-square. Trace letters on to tracing paper, marking the center and adding an underline to use for alignment. Trim and position tracing on top of the pencil lines you have drawn on your board. Anchor with masking tape and transfer with graphite.

Paint letters with a 1/8" One Stroke lettering brush using the color of choice. Pick up a little Faux Art Glaze with your paint. Pull your brush through the paint keeping the hairs flat as you load your brush. Turn your brush over and pull again. Hold your brush on a 45-degree angle as you would a calligraphy pen. Pull strokes to create letters. Do not twist the brush. Hold it at a constant 45-degree angle. Let your brush do the work for you. Move your entire arm and keep pressure constant.

Helpful Hints

Think of these as practice projects. You are learning as you paint. Practice each flower or fruit on a surface such as a glass jar, old crock, cookie tin, coffee can, old book, clay pot, or slate. Paint for the fun of it. Now combine these techniques and paint them on a beautiful tray or box.

Be patient with yourself. Practice makes the difference. If you are not happy with what you have painted then just re-paint it! Rubbing alcohol removes areas of dry acrylic from sealed wood, or simply allow the paint to dry and paint over. Do it again and again, until you are satisfied.

Trace and transfer painting guides as you need to use them. As you practice you will find very quickly that you can freely paint many of these projects. Just transfer the large fruits, birds, cottages, watering cans and areas that you feel need structure. This will allow you to adapt these designs to fit any piece of furniture, wall, or surface. You can paint the whole world.

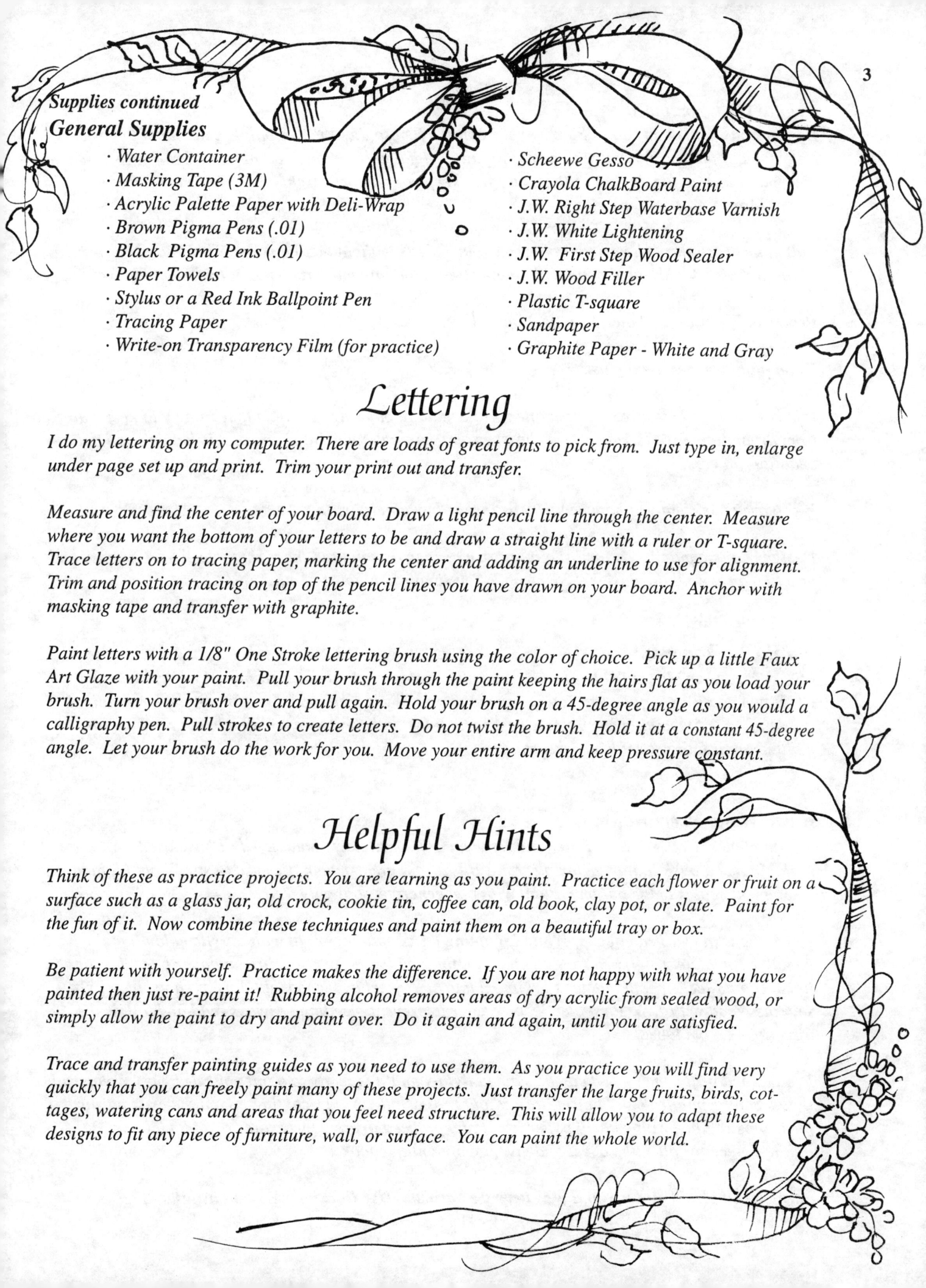

Helpful Hints continued

Be generous with your paint. Pick up your colors often so that there is paint in the tip of the bristle. I have found that I can paint with a very light touch if there is enough paint in my brush. Texture in your paint is a good thing. A little texture will keep your colors bright and creates the shape of a petal. More Paint. More Paint.

Pull your brush through various colors on your palette without mixing them. The colors will form a "Mingled Mess". Mingled paint will create streaks that are more realistic in leaves and flowers.

Practice, Practice, and then Practice some more.

Good paintbrushes are a must.

It is vital that you clean your brush often while you are painting. Frequent cleaning will keep paint from drying up in the ferrule of your brushes and ruining that great shape that is helping you paint beautiful flowers.

If you are consistently unhappy with your results buy a new brush.

Designs can be painted on almost any surface as long as you used the right materials. Get busy and practice on everything in sight. Remember you simply can not ruin a jar.

Paint Chalkboards

I purchased Crayola Chalkboard Paint made by Benjamin Moore in a paint and wallpaper store. Paint two coats on surface and you are ready to go. Always read the direction on the can. Paint the inside of one of your kitchen cabinets doors and it instantly becomes a message board. Varnish only painted areas and not chalkboard surface.

Basic Wood Preparation

Fill any holes with JW Wood Filler and let them dry completely. Sand level. I have used JW White Lightning as a base coat on many pieces as it is also a great sealer. Be sure to stir White Lightning as pigment settles to the bottom. Paint with one generous coat only.

Leave the whitewashed effect of White Lightning or add another coat with acrylic color. Let the base coat dry completely and then sand lightly with fine sandpaper or use a brown paper bag. The final finish should feel smooth but not slick to the touch. If you have wood with lots of knots, then first seal the wood with J. W. First Step Wood Sealer to prevent bleeding. Always read and follow the directions on the label.

Pre-painted or finished wood can be sanded lightly and it is ready to paint your designs. Wonderful things can be painted on old furniture without re-finishing or basecoating. Sand the existing surface, wipe off dust with a damp paper towel and proceed to create treasures. Sand again on top of painted piece to soften the effect and give a more antique look.

Varnish completed pieces with JW Waterbase Varnish. Use Finishing Wax on furniture pieces.

Helpful Hints continued
Crackle Medium

DecoArt makes several types of "Crackle Medium". For background effects I have used Weathered Wood. To create crack on top of painted surface use Perfect Crackle.
Read the manufactures instructions and have fun creating great effects.

Tin or Galvanized Metal

I have had fun painting on unpainted tin and galvanized metal. Just sand lightly and paint your design. Varnish finished piece with Water Based Varnish.

To base with a color the surface must be clean and free of rust. Sand lightly to rough the surface and then spray with a metal primer. Allow primer to dry and paint with two coats of acrylic (spray or brush on) of the desired base color.

Pre-painted metal surfaces, such as mailboxes, should be sanded lightly then painted. Varnish your completed pieces with JW Exterior Waterbase Varnish. Re-varnish as necessary to protect them.

Crocks

Make sure the surface is clean and dry. Paint with DecoArt Multi-Purpose Sealer (DS17) or spray with Krylon Matte Spray (1311). Paint with Americana Acrylic.

Transferring Patterns

Trace pattern on to tracing paper. Position the tracing paper pattern on surface and anchor in place using masking tape. Place graphite paper underneath the tracing paper pattern with dark side down. Transfer basic lines by retracing the pattern using a stylist or ballpoint pen. I like to use a red ballpoint pen so I can see which lines I have traced. Always check as you get started to see that the lines are transferring properly. Take your time; a clear, crisp pattern is worth the extra few minutes.

DecoArt Americana Acrylic paint is used on most of these projects. I love the thickness of this paint and the brilliant colors. I have used DecoArt Faux Glazing Medium with the paint on some of these projects to achieve transparent effects and to aid in blending.

Wet Palette

Place a sheet of deli-wrap (dry wax paper) on top of several layers of wet paper towel or synthetic chamois in a tray or stay-wet box (9" x 12" or larger). Squeeze paint out on top of the damp deli-wrap surface. Paint will stay workable all day. Cover your paint and it will keep for days. The damp surface will keep the paint fresh but will not dilute your paint or allow it to skin over and get gunky. Purchase deli-wrap at party paper stores or warehouse clubs such as Costco or Sam's Club.

Helpful Hints continued
Definitions

Basecoat - *To apply the first layer of color.*

Shading *and* **Highlighting** - *To apply color on top of the base coat, both dark and light, to give dimension to your painting.*

Detailing - *To add fine lines, flower centers, stems, and other touches to give a finished look to your painting.*

Tapping - *To tap very lightly using the tip of the brush, bouncing around rather than moving in straight rows. Use this technique to create foliage or flowers.*

Double Load Brush - *Having two colors in your brush at the same time. First pick up the darker color on the heel of the brush then brush several strokes across the edge of the lighter value loading the point of the brush. Brush in the same places each time you pick up color. The desired effect is t0 have pure color on each edge or corner of the brush and a gradual blending of the two colors in the middle of the brush. I like to have more of my light value and less of the dark in my brush so that the light value will show more and the dark will not take over. I pick up the light value twice as often as the dark. On your deli-wrap palette pick up your color in the same place every time as you are creating a mix on your brush and on the surface of the palette at the same time. This mix will stay wet because of the damp surface so that you can continue to pick it up on your brush as you re-load with your light value.*

Transparent - *Painting with color that has been extended either with water or medium so that you can see through it.*

Antiquing or Glazing - *Used to tint areas of your painted piece to tone and soften. See Creating Special Effects.*

Spattering or Fly Specking - *To tone and soften your painted piece with tiny dots of color.*

Creating Special Effects

Antiquing or Glazing - *Used to tint areas of your painted piece to tone and soften. Pick up Glazing Medium and apply to a area of your painted piece using a 3/4" angle shader. While the Glazing Medium is still wet pick up small amounts of color on the tip of your angle shader and brush across at the edge of your design. You can glaze some of this color on top of your design. The Glazing Medium in the heel of your brush will blend color into the background. Color should be transparent but create a slightly misty effect. If you have too much, quickly wipe off water. Colors can be layered for all types of special effects. Play with soft colors that are in your design adding a little here and there.*

Spattering or Fly Specking - *Thin your paint with water. Use an old toothbrush or any stiff brush you have. Hold brush close to the surface and pull bristles back with your finger to make spatters of paint fly. Always test first on a scrap. Use colors from your design.*

Painting Flowers

I fill my brush full so that I can stroke and tap with a light touch to achieve a delicate look.

Practice the flowers on "Write On" Transparency Film (Office Supply stores). Paint over the worksheet in the books by laying the piece of film on top. Make a notebook of your own flower studies.

*Paint background foliage first with **Avocado**, **Evergreen**, **Olive Green**, and **Blue Mist**. Let it dry. Pattern or sketch with a white chalk pencil on top of the foliage. Try free handing these flowers using your pattern only as a visual guide for positioning. Paint main flowers next, add leaves, filler flowers, stems and squiggles. Put these flowers together as they please you. Remember you are painting your own gardens. Test colors first on transparency film and lay on top to check color and position. Try out colors on a jar or tin can.*

Daisies

*Use a round brush, size will vary according to the size of your petals. Most of my daises are painted with a #2 round brush. Load your brush by pulling through the puddle of **Titanium White** several times. Start your daisy with the center, touching down with the side of the brush to form an oval. Pull each petal in from the edge as in the illustration starting with the tip of the brush handle straight up. Push down gently on the brush and pull toward the center, lifting as you pull. Vary the length of your petals. Petals #1 and #2 are the longest. Complete all your daisies; add calyxes and stems using one of your shades of green. Paint centers with **Cadmium Yellow**. Shade lower section with a mix of **Cadmium Yellow** and **Burnt Sienna**.*

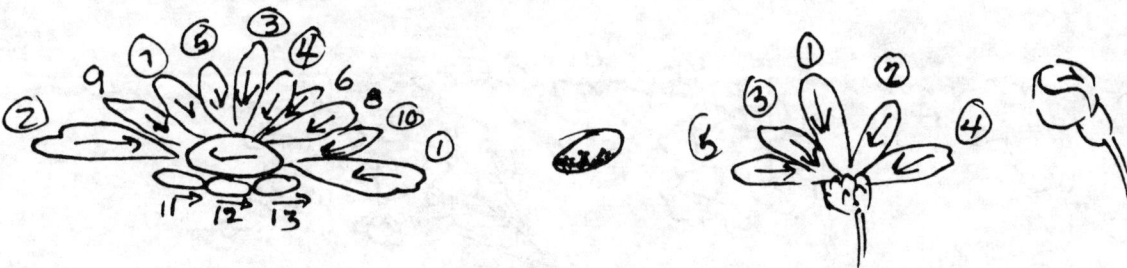

Tulips

*Base in oval shaped flower with filbert brush (size determined by the size of flower) using **Royal Fuchsia** and **Titanium White**. Highlight the top of the tulip with a lighter shade of **Titanium White** and **Royal Fuchsia** using one or two strokes. Tulip leaves are fat blade shapes created by pulling up strokes with various shades of green. Paint yellow tulips with **Antique Gold**, **Cadmium Yellow**, **Lemon Yellow** and **Titanium White**.*

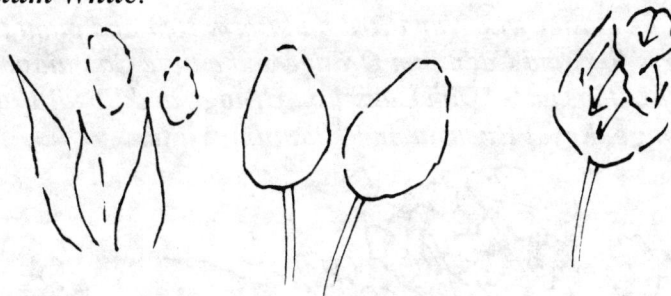

8

Roses

I found I liked my roses best when I paint them with simple loose shapes. If they get too fussy I just mess them up a bit.

*Creamy Roses: Load your brush by touching the heel of the brush into **Raw Sienna** and tip of the brush into **Buttermilk** (double loaded brush). Stroke flat on your palette in the edge of the light value. Paint two rows of petals inside of the cup of the flower and two rows on the outside, hold the brush horizontal with the tip up and stroke up, across and down to create a petal. Lay your brush flat so that you are using the back of the brush. Lift your brush and set it back down to give the illusion of many petals instead of just one large petal. Paint extra rows around the outside to create more open roses. Paint calyx and stem on rose buds with **Glazing Medium**, **Avocado** and **Blue Mist** using your #2 round brush.*

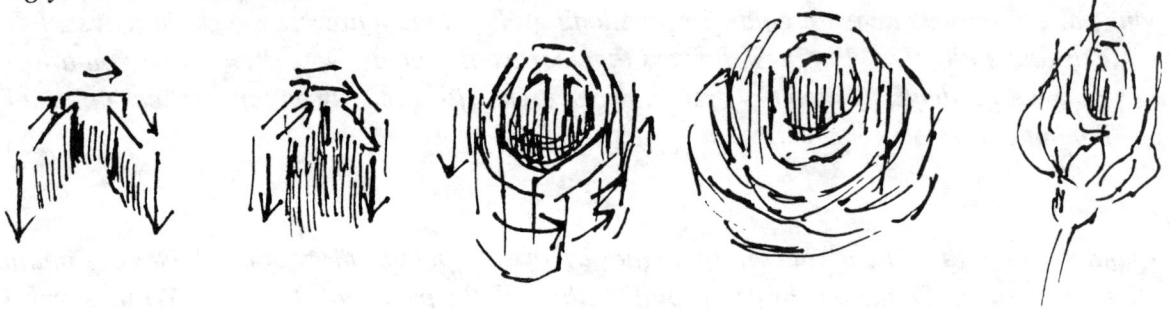

Lilacs

*Paint these flowers with a round or filbert brush (size is determined by the size of the flower) by pulling through **Dioxazine Purple**, **Blue Violet** and **Titanium White**. Apply dabs of color. Pull brush through the edge of more **Titanium White** and paint four petal flowers on top of the wet base of color. Vary the color and shape of these cluster flowers. Paint more pastel flowers by adding some **Glazing Medium** to the undercoat of color. Add a few stems peeking through the petals with **Olive Green**. Paint some dots of **Olive Green** and **Titanium White** to create buds.*

Geraniums

Geraniums are painted on wet base of color. Dab on base colors and while still wet pick up lighter values and pull four petal flowers forming a loose oval. Pick up paints by pulling through the edge of colors to create streaky colors. Ridges in your paint will help create the flowers. Leave some spaces to peek some stems through.

*Red Geraniums: Base the cluster with **Napa Red** and **Berry Red** and paint three and four petal flowers on top with **Berry Red** and **Cadmium Orange** and a little **Cadmium Yellow**.*

*Salmon Geraniums: Base the cluster with **Cadmium Orange** and **Royal Fuchsia**. Paint flowers on top with **Cadmium Orange**, **Royal Fuchsia** and **Titanium White**.*

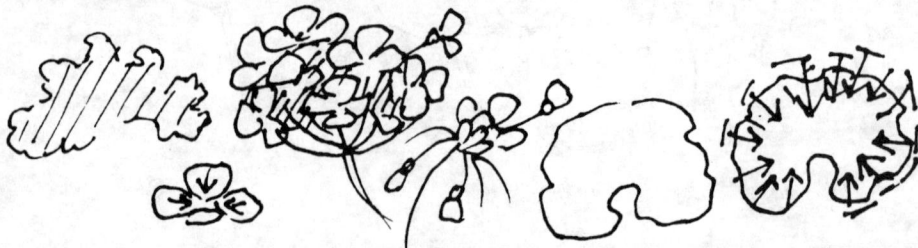

**CREAMY ROSES
CURVED TOP TRUNK
ROS'S PAINT BOX
WOODEN COAT HANGER
PAGES 28 - 37, 42 - 43**

Creamy Roses

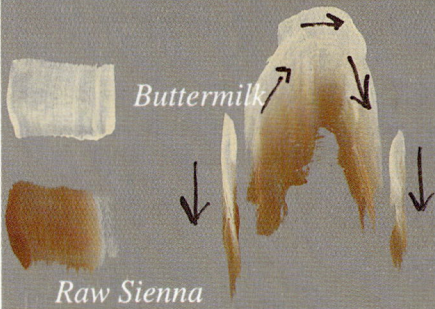

Buttermilk

Raw Sienna

1/2" Angle Shader

Row 1

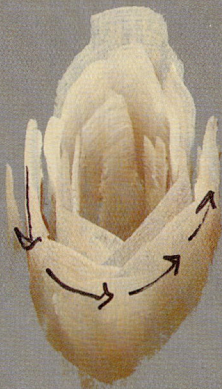

Row 2

Row 3

Row 4

Base filler flowers with Olive Green Paint flowers with Titanium White

Paint Calyx with Avocado, Blue Mist & Glazing Medium

Viburnum

Viburnum or Snowball bush bloom early spring with white or pink ball shaped clusters of blossoms. Dab **Glazing Medium** and **Olive Green** oval. Add a little **Blue Mist** near the stem end. While still wet pull four little petal flowers with **Titanium White** using a #4 filbert brush. Let the undercoat color pick up as you create the blossoms. Pick up fresh paint only once or twice so that you have lots of variation. Keep shapes uneven to keep a loose look.

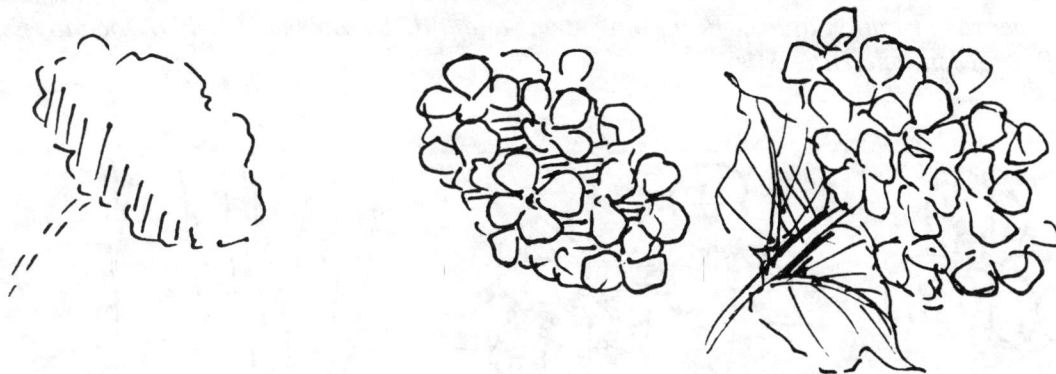

Poinsettias

Poinsettias are red leaves and the flowers are really the little dots in the center! Base petals with **Berry Red** using 1/2" angle shader. Highlight with **Cadmium Orange** and **Cadmium Orange** mixed with a little **Titanium White**. Shade along the center vein on one side and separate the petals with **Napa Red**. Deepen value here and there by adding a little **Dioxazine Purple**. Work with lots of paint since these are transparent colors. Paint veins with **Napa Red** and water using a liner brush. Dot the center with **Cadmium Yellow** using the end of a paintbrush. Add a **Berry Red** smaller dot on top of the **Cadmium Yellow** dot.

Black Eyed Susans & Sunflowers

Black Eyed Susans and Sunflowers are similar. Sunflowers are much larger and the centers grow to be huge by late summer as the seeds ripen. As the centers grow the petals twist and curl. Many of the heads turn downward. Black Eyed Susans have puffy centers that sit up. Overstroke the petals with two strokes to give the illusion of the fold in the petal.

Paint flower centers and petals with **Antique Gold** using a round. Tap centers with **Burnt Umber** and **Burnt Sienna** using a few hairs on the tip of 1/2" Foliage Brush. Strengthen color at base of center (and in the middle of the center of the Sunflowers) with **Paynes Grey**. Paint second row of petals with **Cadmium Yellow** allowing some of the base color to show. Highlight some of the petals with **Lemon Yellow**.

12

Iris

*Paint a comma stroke from the right with **Dioxazine Purple** and **Titanium White** using a filbert brush. Paint second stroke overlapping the first on the left side. Paint center petal from the bottom up by mashing filbert brush flat and wiggling hairs to make them fan out then slide up and to the chisel edge of the brush to form petal. Pull two side petals up from the bottom up. Add a second stroke on these side petals as needed. Tap little **Cadmium Yellow** dots with the tip of your liner to create Iris beards or pollen areas. Paint long stems and tall slender leaves with **Avocado, Evergreen, Olive Green,** and **Blue Mist**.*

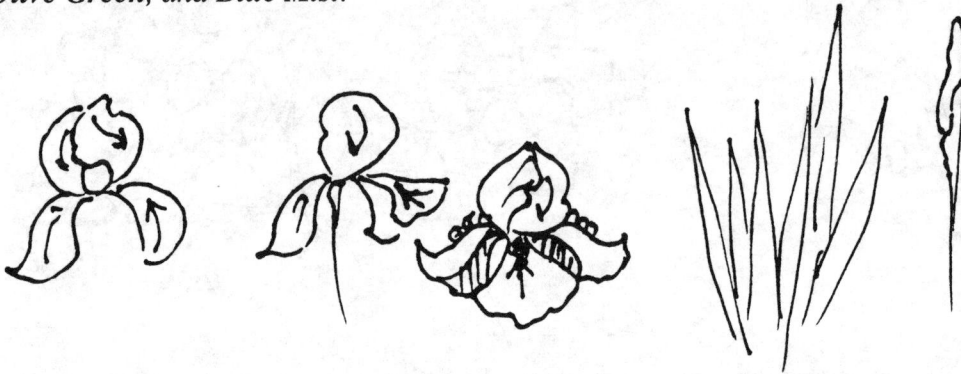

Queen Anne's Lace

*Paint Queen Anne's Lace with your 3/4" foliage brush. Tap loose oval shapes with **Olive Green**. Add some taps of **Blue Mist** along the lower edge and on one side. Tap highlight of **Lemon Yellow** on the upper left. Tap **Titanium White** over this base of color; do not cover the entire base. Paint dots and four petal flowers at random over the white areas. Paint stems with **Olive Green** (adjust the color for contrast by adding **Pineapple, Lemon Yellow** or **Avocado**). Spatter with **Titanium White**.*

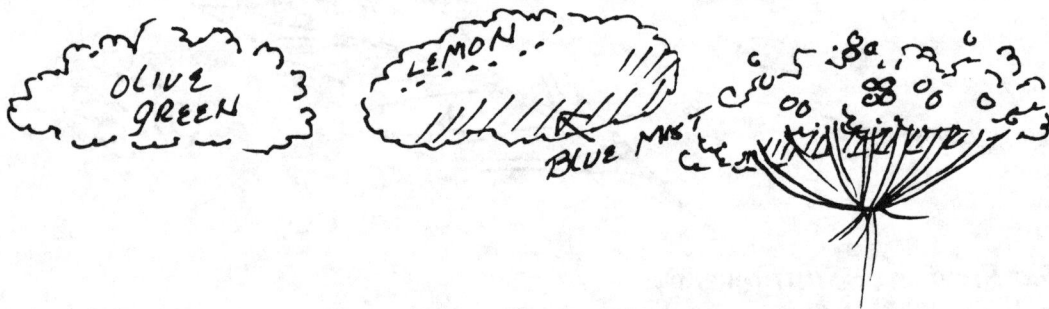

Ferns

*Tap ferns with the edge of a 2/0 fan brush using various shades of green and **Glazing Medium**. Paint some little balls on the ends of some fronds. Think of curved fir trees.*

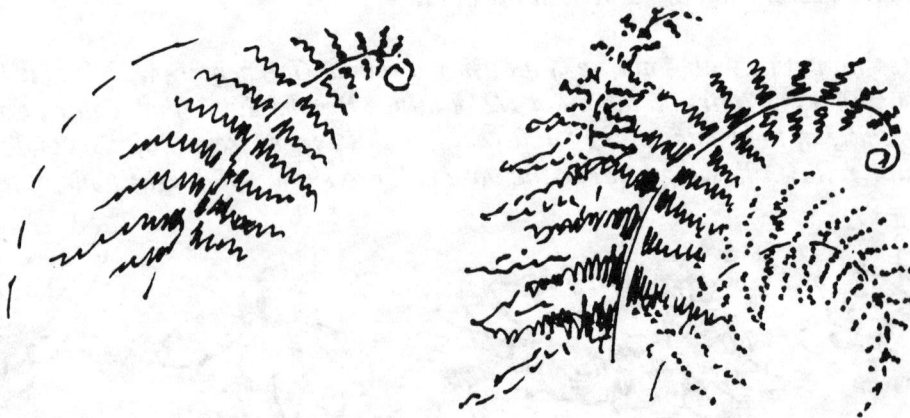

Bamboo

*Create bamboo stalks with edge of 1/2" angle shader varing the colors using **Glazing Medium**, **Avocado**, **Evergreen**, **Raw Sienna** and touches of **Dioxazine Purple**.*

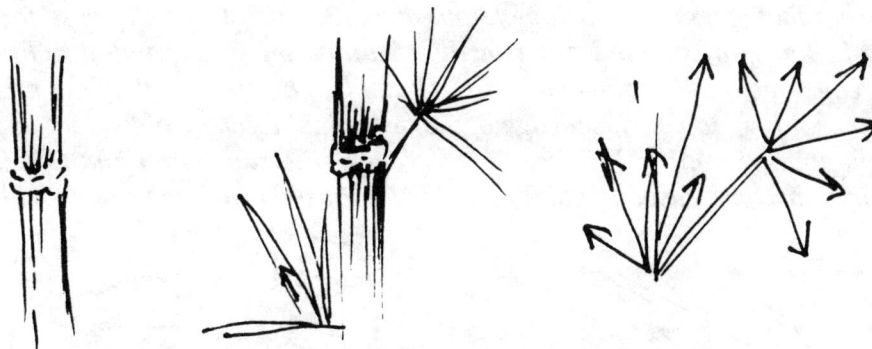

Ribbons

*Paint ribbons any color you wish to complement your design. I used a 1/2" angle shader brush. Select two values of a color. Base in ribbon with the lighter value and **Glazing Medium**. Start with the brush horizontal and fix your hand so that you do not turn your fingers and move your whole arm. Let your brush do the work. Start stroke with light pressure, apply some pressure and lift as you pull toward the end of the stroke. This will create thicks and thins to make the ribbon look as if it turns and twists. Practice, Practice.*

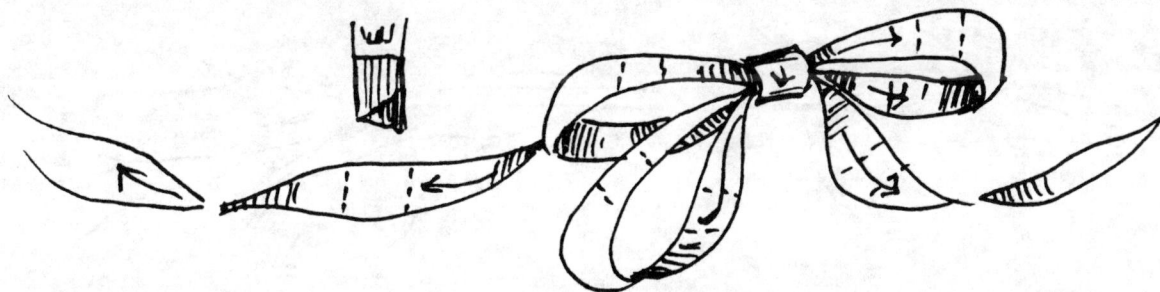

*You can create simple bows and streamers using this same method. Pick up your paint by pulling the flat of the brush through fresh paint. Pick up your paint often so that it will flow as you pull your brush. Remove strokes with a damp paper towel if it gets away from you and simply do it over again. Highlight ribbon in widest places with double loaded brush with base color and **White**. Shade narrow places with double loaded brush with base color and dark value. Brush highlight and shading color across the ribbon.*

Basic Leaves

*Basic leaves are a sloppy triangle shape. Base in leaves with **Avocado** using your angle shader. Darken one side of the center of each leaf with **Evergreen** using the point of your angle shader. Highlight with **Olive Green** and **Blue Mist**.*

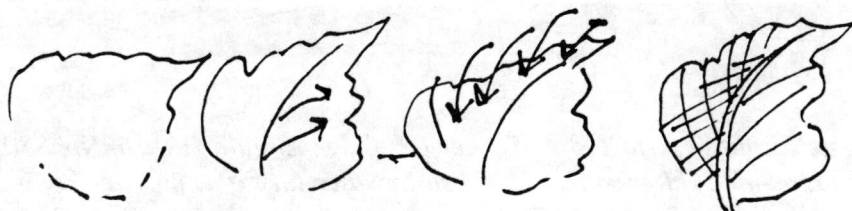

Squishy Leaves

*These leaves are called squishy leaves because you create them by simply squishing the paint from underneath your brush. Paint squishy leaves with any combination of shades of green using a flat brush. Remember that you must have a generous amount of paint in your brush for it to squish out to form this leaf. Touch brush into **Faux Glazing Medium** and fresh paint, turn brush and pat again, tip one edge into another shade of green. Paint leaf by pushing the flat of the brush sideways across the surface, lift up to the chisel edge of the brush in the center of the leaf and slip it forward to make a slight point. Practice, Practice, and Practice. Pick up more **Faux Glazing Medium** to create transparent leaves. I usually paint three leaves together and add a stem with a liner brush.*

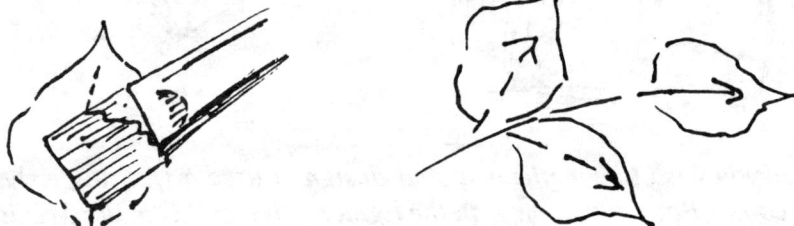

Branches

*Paint branches with a wash of **Burnt Umber** using your liner brush. Load brush fully with water and paint. Work brush in paint to load and roll back to a point. Start branch at largest end, apply pressure and pull toward smaller branches. Wiggle your brush slightly as you pull to create small twigs.*

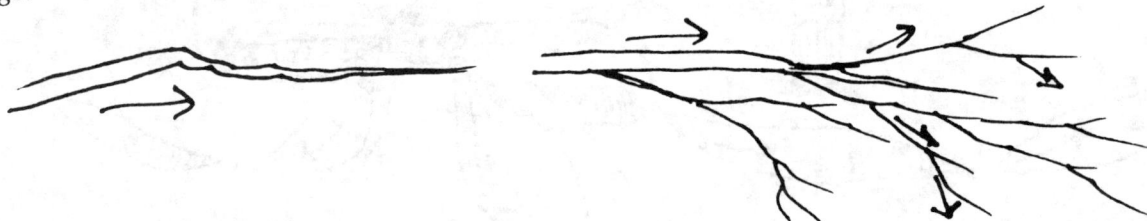

Stems & Squiggles

Paint stems and squiggles with your liner brush. Pick up your paint with a little water; pull your brush through the paint a few times to load it fully with this wet mixture. Balance your brush hand on your other hand. The handle of the brush should be pointing straight up. Touch only the tip of the brush to the surface and use a delicate, light touch.

Pull the tip of the brush toward you applying as little pressure as possible. This will create a narrow fluid line something like ink from a pen. Practice swirling the brush by stiffening your wrist and moving your entire arm to form squiggles.

Foliage & Trees

Tap foliage with Suzie's Foliage Brush (3/4" Scheewe Foliage Angular Brush, No. S8037, Martin F. Weber) and any of your shades of green. Soak brush in water for a few minutes before using to let the hairs of the brush fluff out. Tap bristles on your palette to open hairs. Tip only the front half of the hairs into fresh paint and tap lightly on your palette. The point of the brush is up and tip the handle forward so as to use only the forward hairs. Tap gently on the surface to create foliage. Many light taps are best, turning the brush in different directions. Stop when you have created a nice lacy appearance.

Foliage & Trees continued

*Paint tree trunks with **Burnt Umber** and a little water, using your No. 0 Liner Brush. Start with the trunk and lift up to form branches.*

Fir Trees

*Tap fir or evergreen trees with the edge of a small 2/0 or 1/0 fan brush using **Black Green** and **Antique Teal** (lighten with background color and **Glazing Medium** for distant trees). Tap trunk line and begin below the top of the line to form branches. Keep the top of the tree tiny and begin to widen as you work toward the bottom. Use only about 1/2 of the brush tapping lightly work back and forth across covering the trunk line. Leave open ragged edges for the best results. Tap snow on branches with **Winter Blue** and the **Hi-Lite Flesh**.*

Painting Fruit

*Start all of the large fruits by painting a basecoat. Highlight the basecoat with **Titanium White** and the base color by loading the heel of 1/2" angle shader with **Titanium White** and the tip of the brush with the base color. Pat with the flat of the brush keeping the point of the brush with the base to the outer edge of the fruit. Allow colors to dry between layers. If you get carried away simply add some of the base color. Glaze fruits with **Faux Glazing Medium** in the heel of your brush and pigment in the point. Touch the heel of brush into **Glazing Medium** and slide the tip of brush across the edge of pigment a couple of times to load paint half way across the bristles. The first glazing color goes all the way around the fruit. Each color thereafter covers less of the area. Look closely at the color step-by-step directions.*

Glaze over entire surface at least two times as you add layers, this will give depth to the fruit. Glazing medium does not extend the drying time. It can be removed by wiping off with water while it is still wet. Once a layer is dry the next layer will not lift the color. Paint each layer quickly, let dry and add another layer. If your paint begins to feel sticky allow to dry and add more layers. Sometimes you need to have a little more paint in your brush so that the surface dries slower. Learn to stop. Leave some of each color showing.

16

Pears

*Undercoat pears on dark backgrounds with **Titanium White**. Paint with **Cadmium Yellow**. Highlight with **Titanium White**. Glaze pears first with **Antique Gold**. Progress to darker values using **Raw Sienna, Burnt Sienna, Cadmium Orange** and **Olive Green**. Strengthen highlight with dabs of **Titanium White** and **Lemon Yellow**. Paint stem with **Burnt Umber** and highlight with **Raw Sienna** and **Titanium White**. Spatter with **Emperors Gold**.*

Red Apples

*Undercoat apples with **Titanium White** on dark backgrounds. Paint with **Cadmium Orange**. Highlight with **Titanium White** and **Cadmium Orange**. Wet the surface of the apple with water and **Berry Red** streak from the smile line down and from the bottom up on the damp surface. Glaze across the top and down the left side with **Napa Red**. Deepen the color down in the core with **Napa Red**. Wet the surface again and pull streaks on the right side in toward the core with **Olive Green** using the tip of 1/2" angle shader. Add strong highlights with **Titanium White**. Paint stems with **Burnt Umber** and **Titanium White**. Spatter with **Emperors Gold**.*

*Paint apple slices with **Buttermilk** and shade with **Raw Sienna** and touches of **Olive Green**. Paint seed with **Burnt Umber**. Paint edges like the apple.*

Royal Gala

*Paint Royal Gala apples with a base of **Cadmium Yellow** and pull streaks like on the Red apples.*

Green Apples

*Undercoat apples with **Titanium White** on dark backgrounds. Paint with **Olive Green**. Highlight with **Titanium White**, **Olive Green** and **Lemon Yellow**. Glaze with **Blue Mist**, **Lemon Yellow** and **Cadmium Orange**. Deepen stem or blossom end with **Evergreen**. Paint stem with **Burnt Umber** and highlight with **Burnt Umber** and **Titanium White**. Spatter with **Emperor's Gold**.*

Yellow Apples

Paint yellow apples with the same colors as if it were a pear.

Berries

*Paint these berries with a cotton swab. Sue Scheewe taught me this technique some years ago and I have had more fun painting them. It works great for blackberries, raspberries, holly berries, small grapes, pyracantha berries, and bittersweet. Let your imagination work for you. For smaller berries pull some of the cotton off the end of your swab. (Inexpensive cotton swabs work great as they usually have less cotton the tip.) Touch cotton swab into **Faux Glazing Medium** and roll the tip in your fingers to reshape it before taping in the paint. Touch one edge into a color and tip the other edge into another. A hole should form in the middle of the berry. As the swab gets ragged on the edges roll the edges back into shape on the palette. My little granddaughter, Paige, loves to use her finger so now I also paint "finger berries". To create large berries try tapping into paint with the ends of wooden dowels of various sizes. Be generous with your paint and tap into various colors.*

Green Berries

*Paint large green berries with 3/8"angle shader. Base berries with **Olive Green**. Load brush with **Faux Glazing Medium** in the heel of brush and color on the point only. Glaze left side of berry with **Blue Mist** and **Colonial Green**. Add some **Evergreen** near the bottom and to create the little "U" depression for the stem. Highlight on the right side and under the stem with **Pineapple**. Paint a little curved line for the shine with **Titanium White**. Paint stem with **Burnt Umber**.*

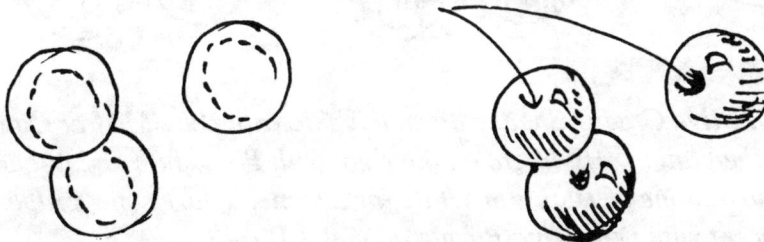

Strawberries

*Undercoat berries with **Titanium White** on dark backgrounds. Paint basecoat of **Cadmium Orange** on all strawberries using an angle shader (size determined by the size of your berries). Highlight the center of each berry with **Titanium White**. Paint diagonal lines with **Titanium White** using your liner brush across the berries forming diamond shapes to create the segments for the seeds. Paint little curved lines to round the corners of segments. Paint seeds with **Olive Green** and paint a little line down the left side of each seed with **Evergreen**. Allow to dry. Glaze the berries with **Faux Glazing Medium** and **Cadmium Orange** all the way around the outside of each berry. Allow each layer of glaze and color to dry before adding another layer. Glaze **Berry Red** across the top, down the left side and across the bottom of each berry. Glaze **Napa Red** across the top and across the bottom of each berry. Paint caps of each berry with small squishy leaves using **Avocado**, **Evergreen** and **Olive Green**. Strengthen the color in a few places on the left side by glazing with **Black Plum**. Accent some berries on the right side with **Olive Green** to create some unripe berries.*

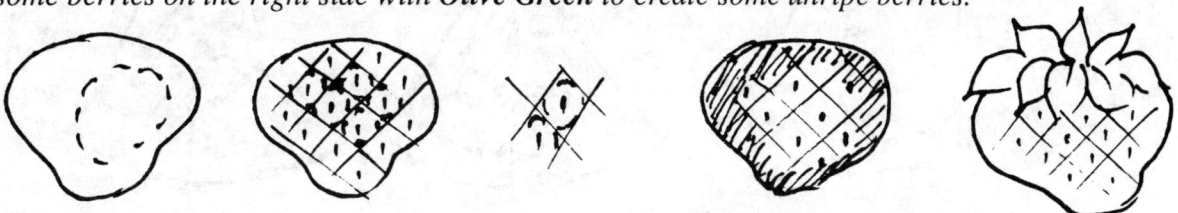

Cherries

*Paint cherries with **Cadmium Orange**. Shade with **Napa Red**, **Berry Red** and **Dioxazine Purple**. Highlight with **Cadmium Orange** and **Titanium White**. Accent with **Royal Fuchsia**. For quick cherries tap a 3/4" wooden dowel into color and press to surface. Let dry and accent with **Royal Fuchsia** and highlight with **Cadmium Orange** and **Titanium White**.*

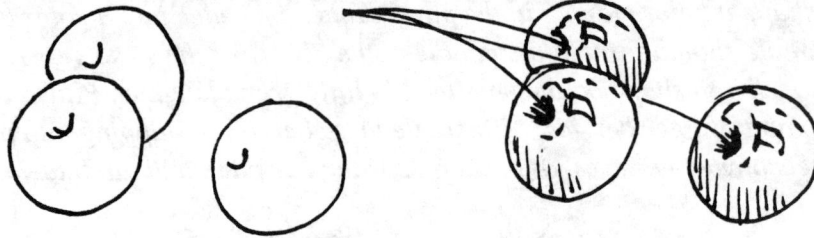

Red Grapes

*I painted these grapes with **Cadmium Orange**. Shade with **Black Plum**. Accent wedge shape with **Berry Red**. Highlight with **Cadmium Orange** and **Titanium White** on the right side. Paint **Country Blue** on the left side. Paint bright **Titanium White** shine highlights. Paint stems with **Burnt Umber** and **Raw Sienna**.*

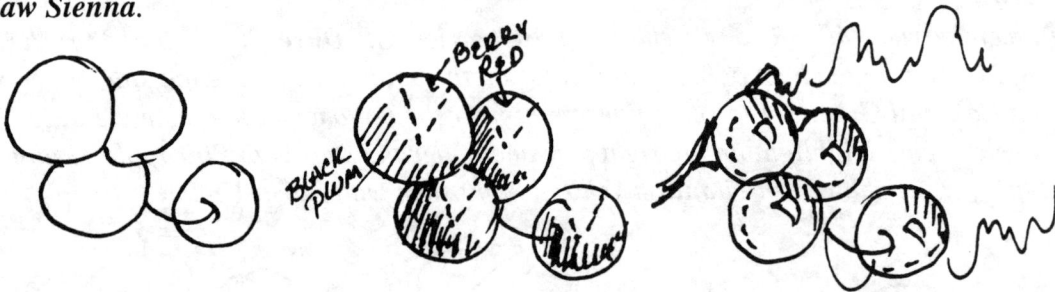

Green Grapes

*Paint green grapes with **Olive Green**. Shaded down left side with **Blue Mist** or **Colonial Green**. Add **Evergreen** across the bottom. Highlight on the right with **Pineapple** and a touch of **Lemon Yellow**. Paint a little curved line of **Titanium White** for a shine. Glaze some grapes with a little **Cadmium Orange**. Accent with **Dioxazine Purple** or **Violet Haze**.*

Watermelon

*Undercoat watermelons with **Titanium White** on dark backgrounds. Paint with **Cadmium Orange**, **Royal Fuchsia** and **Titanium White**. Double load your 1/2" angular shader with **Titanium White** on the point and **Cadmium Orange** and **Titanium White** on the heel of the brush. Brush across the outer edge to create the rind. Paint the edge with **Evergreen**. Pat in a few darker areas for seeds with **Faux Glazing Medium** and **Napa Red**. Paint seeds with **Ivory Black** and highlight with **Titanium White**. Lighten a few places in front of the seeds to set them in with **Cadmium Orange** and **Titanium White**. Keep shapes irregular.*

CREAMY ROSES
DESK ACCESSORIES
SCISSOR HOLDER
SMALL BOX
PAGES 28 - 37, 42 - 43

Basket

*Paint the basic shape of the basket with **Burnt Umber**. Paint vertical lines with **Raw Sienna** using the edge of an angle shader or flat brush. Paint horizontal lines with **Raw Sienna** and **Camel** starting at the far left according to the diagram to form the weave of the basket.*

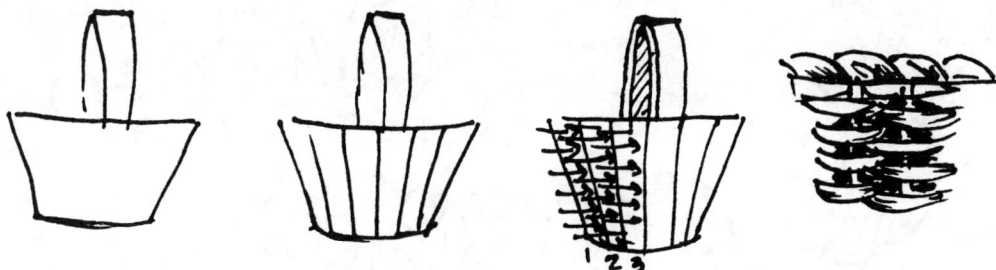

Feed the Birds

Surface: Small Metal Trashcan (Target), Tall Wooden Box (Country Crafts)

Palette: DecoArt Americana Acrylic

DA001 Titanium White	DA014 Cadmium Orange	DA019 Berry Red
DA052 Avocado	DA056 Olive Green	DA064 Burnt Umber
DA067 Lamp Black	DA068 Slate Grey	DA079 Brandy Wine
DA082 Evergreen	DA093 Raw Sienna	DA148 Emperor Gold
DA153 Eggshell	DA165 Napa Red	DA172 Black Plum
DA178 Blue Mist	Faux Glazing Medium	

Preparation: Metal Trashcan, Sand and wipe with rubbing alcohol. Tall Wooden Box, base with a mix of **Eggshell** and **Glazing Medium**.

Branches: Paint branches with a brush mix of **Burnt Umber**, **Emperor's Gold** and **Glazing Medium** using a liner brush.

Squishy Leaves: Paint squishy leaves with **Evergreen**, **Avocado**, **Olive Green**, **Blue Mist**, **Emperor's Gold** and **Glazing Medium**, using assorted sizes of flat shaders.

Pattern: Trace and transfer birds and lettering with gray graphite. Position birds on any branch and you can add another branch.

Chickadees: Paint with **Titanium White**, **Slate Grey**, **Lamp Black** and **Raw Sienna**.

Cardinal: Paint with **Brandy Wine**, **Napa Red**, **Lamp Black**, **Raw Sienna**, **Cadmium Orange** and **Berry Red**.

Lettering: Paint lettering with **Brandy Wine** and line down the right side with **Black Plum** using 1/8" One Stroke lettering brush.

Berries: Paint berries with **Black Plum**, **Brandy Wine**, **Cadmium Orange** and **Glazing Medium** using Q-Tips. Highlight berries with **Titanium White** using a liner brush.

Feed the Birds
Small Metal Trashcan

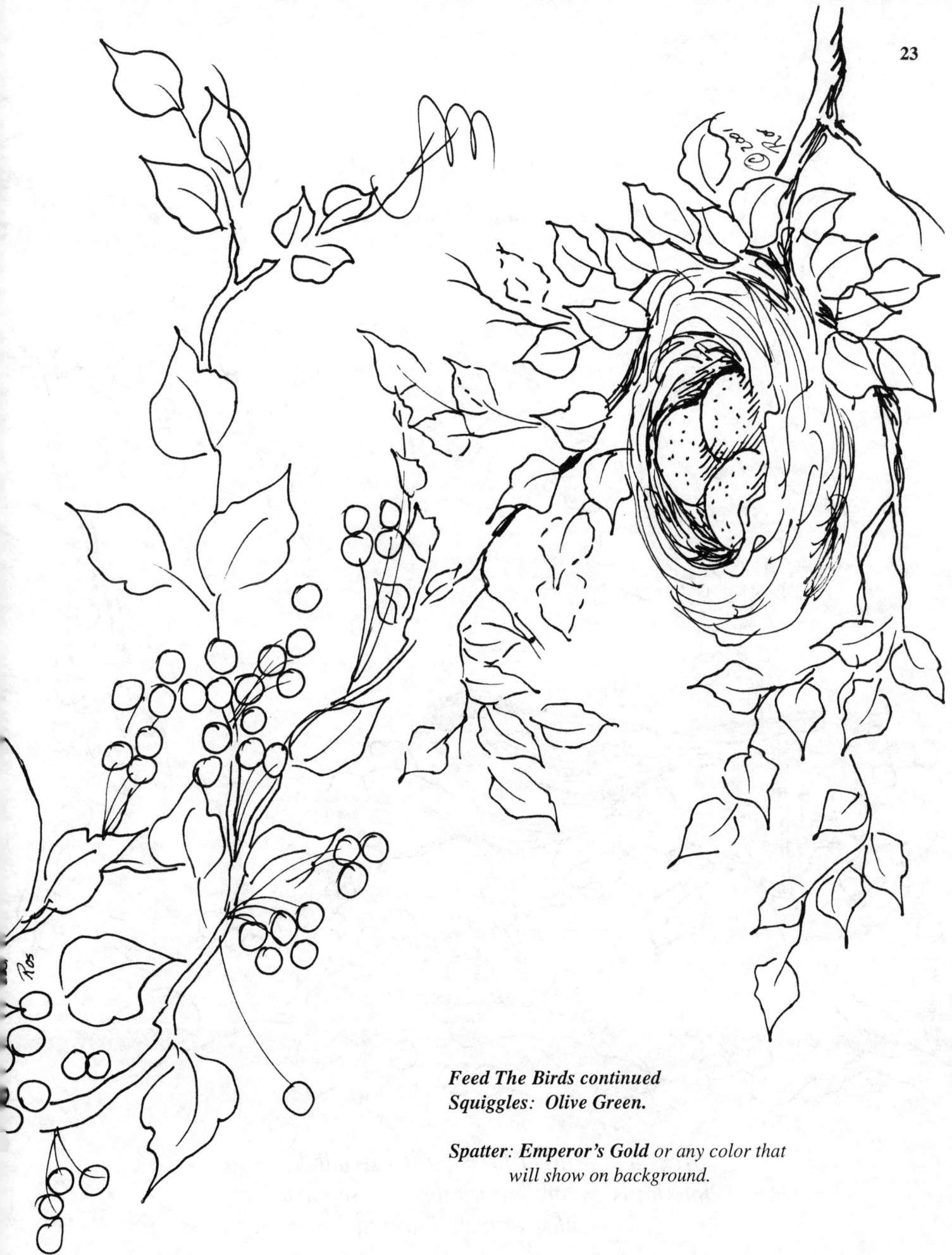

Feed The Birds continued
Squiggles: Olive Green.

Spatter: Emperor's Gold *or any color that*
will show on background.

Feed the Birds
Tall Wooden Box

Trace and transfer these birds carefully.
Place birds on any branch that pleases you.
Add another branch if needed.

I love to watch these little chickadees in my backyard. I like to paint birds like I see them at my feeders, rather than how they appear in field guides.

Feed the Birds - Cardinals and Apples

Surface: *Wooden Turntable (Lavender Cat)*

Palette: *DecoArt Americana Acrylic*

DA001 Titanium White	*DA014 Cadmium Orange*	*DA019 Berry Red*
DA052 Avocado	*DA056 Olive Green*	*DA064 Burnt Umber*
DA067 Lamp Black	*DA079 Brandy Wine*	*DA082 Evergreen*
DA093 Raw Sienna	*DA101 Dioxazine Purple*	*DA148 Emperor's Gold*
DA152 Shale Green	*DA165 Napa Red*	*DA167 Paynes Gray*
DA178 Blue Mist	*Faux Glazing Medium*	

Basecoat: *Shale Green edge with* **Emperor's Gold.**

Pattern: *Trace and transfer pattern of leaves, cardinal and apples using gray graphite.*

Branches: **Burnt Umber** *and* **Glazing Medium.** *Paint pale squishy leaves with various shades of Greens and a lot of* **Glazing Medium.**

Leaves: *Base leaves with* **Avocado.** *Highlight with* **Olive Green** *and* **Blue Mist** *using 1/2" angle shader. Shade leaves with* **Evergreen.**

Cardinal: *Paint with* **Brandy Wine, Napa Red, Lamp Black, Raw Sienna, Cadmium Orange** *and* **Berry Red.**

Apples: *Paint apples with* **Cadmium Orange, Berry Red, Napa Red, Olive Green** *and* **Burnt Umber.**

Finishing Touches: *Paint squiggles and spatter with* **Emperor's Gold.**

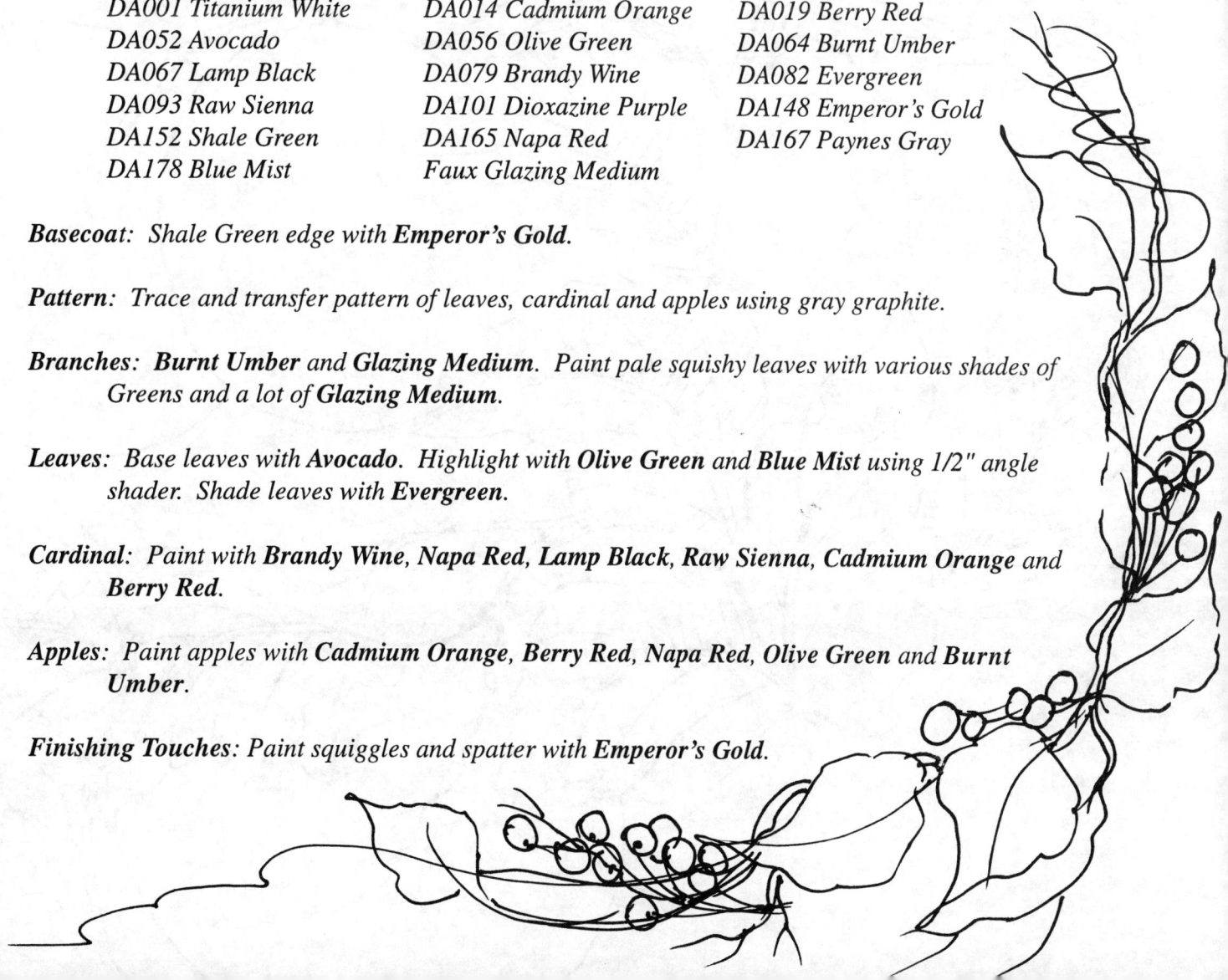

Feed the Birds
Cardinals and Apples
Wooden Turntable

Fill you tin with sunflower
seeds just for the Cardinals
and Chickadees.

Try painting different varieties of apples.
Techniques are the same. Pull streaks on apples
with the corner of a mini fan brush.

Creamy Roses

Surfaces: *Curved Top Trunk, Desk Accessories - Ros's Paint Box (Russ Hayden),
Scissors Holder (Stan Brown's Arts & Crafts) Small Box, Wooden Coat Hanger*

Palette: *DecoArt Americana*
DA001 Titanium White	*DA003 Buttermilk*	*DA052 Avocado*
DA056 Olive Green	*DA082 Evergreen*	*DA148 Emperor's Gold*
DA158 Antique Teal	*DA093 Raw Sienna*	*DA178 Blue Mist*
DA218 Gingerbread	*Faux Glazing Medium*	

Basecoat: White Lightning.

Foliage: Avocado Evergreen, Olive Green and **Blue Mist.**

Squishy Leaves: *Paint squishy leaves with* **Glazing Medium, Evergreen, Avocado, Blue Mist** *and* **Emperor's Gold.**

Roses: Buttermilk, Raw Sienna, Olive Green, *and sometimes a little* **Gingerbread.**

Filler Flowers: *Paint little four petal flowers at random on wet* **Olive Green** *and* **Glazing Medium** *background with* **Titanium White.**

Ribbons: *Paint ribbon with* **Glazing Medium** *and* **Blue Mist.** *Shade with* **Antique Teal** *and highlight with* **Titanium White.** *Ribbons on the coat hanger and small box,* **Gingerbread** *and* **Titanium White.**

Stems *and* **Squiggles: Emperor's Gold.**

Spatter *and* **Edge of Box: Emperor's Gold.**

Background Tints: *Glaze over edge of flowers with* **Glazing Medium** *and* **Blue Mist** *to soften effect.*

Creamy Roses
Left side of Letter Tray

*Brighten your desk or computer table with these beautiful
accessories. Paint a tin can, flowerpot or jar to hold pencils.*

LILACS
MEDIUM OVAL BOARD
PAGES 41, 44 - 45

DOMINO BOX
PAGES 47 - 48

Viburnum

Titanium White

Olive Green

Blue Mist

Avocado

Evergreen

Violet Haze

Blue Violet

Dioxazine Purple

Base with
Olive Green &
Blue Mist +
Glazing
Medium

Pull petals on
wet surface
with #4 Filbert&
Titanium White

Accent with
Violet Haze
Add stems &
leaves

Lilac

Dab base with
Dioxazine Purple &
Blue Violet
with Glazing Medium

Pull 4 petal flowers
with Titanium White

Add stems & buds
with Olive Green

Creamy Roses
Letter Tray

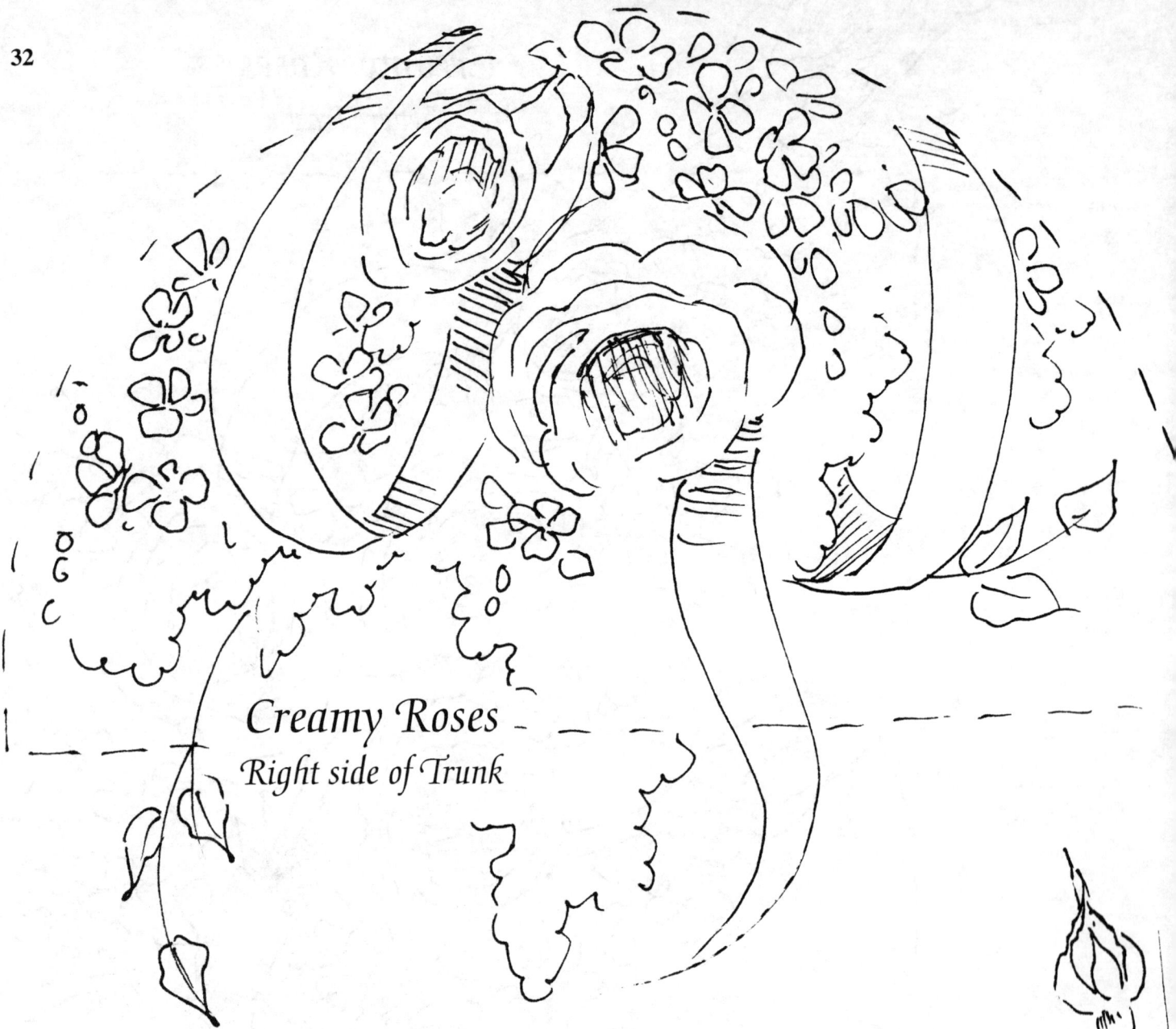

Creamy Roses
Right side of Trunk

Creamy Roses
Mini Oval Box

Creamy Roses
Left side of Trunk

Practice painting these roses be laying
Write-On Transparency Film on top of the worksheet
and actually paint the worksheet step by step.
Try different colors and lay them on top of your piece
to check colors.

Creamy Roses
Top of Trunk

*Paige & Caroline would love one of these
little trunks to keep their treasures in.*

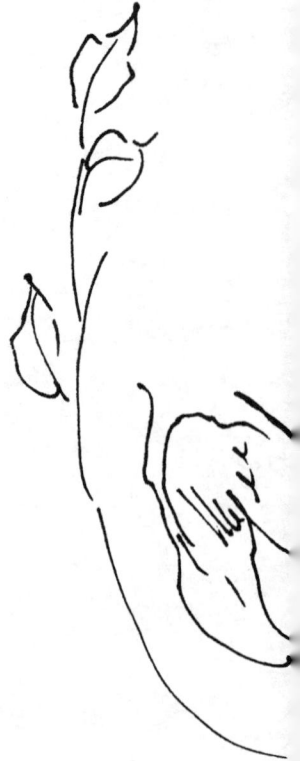

Thank You

Bottom Front

Creamy Roses
Ros's Paint Box

When painting these Roses pick up your paint
often and use a light touch. Lift your brush and
put it back down to create the look of many petals
instead of one large petal.

The girls and I spend great times
out in my studio.
I plan to start roses next.

Tea Time

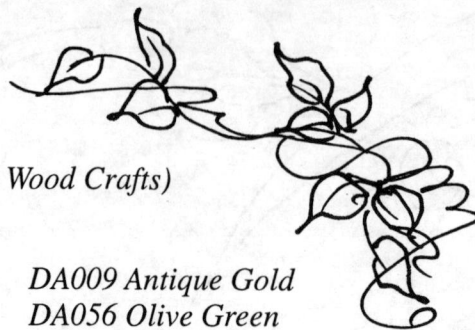

Surface: Tea Box (Lavender Cat or Allen Wood Crafts)

Palette: DecoArt Americana Acrylic

DA001 Titanium White	DA003 Buttermilk	DA009 Antique Gold
DA010 Cadmium Yellow	DA052 Avocado	DA056 Olive Green
DA082 Evergreen	DA093 Raw Sienna	DA153 Eggshell
DA158 Antique Teal	DA162 Antique Mauve	DA167 Paynes Grey
DA178 Blue Mist	Faux Glazing Medium	

Basecoats: Paint tea box with one coat of **White Lightning**. Sand lightly.

Pattern: Trace and lightly transfer pattern for the lettering, teacup, saucer, and edge of napkin using gray graphite. Sand over the design lightly to remove some of the graphite.

Vines: Paint pale vines with **Raw Sienna** and water using your #2/0 liner brush.

Squishy Leaves: Paint pale squishy leaves with **Glazing Medium**, **Avocado**, **Evergreen**, and **Blue Mist** using #12 and #6 flat shaders. Vary the colors and keep pale and distant.

Teacup: Base teacup with **Buttermilk**. Shade with **Paynes Grey** and highlight with **Titanium White**. Paint tea in cup with **Raw Sienna** mixed with **Glazing Medium**. Shade along the sides and along the bottom edge with a little **Paynes Grey** and **Glazing Medium**. Paint rims with **Cadmium Yellow** in the center and **Antique Gold** sides. Deepen values on the edges with **Raw Sienna**. Add **Titanium White** highlight in the center of yellow areas. Paint line under rims with **Glazing Medium** and **Paynes Grey** using a liner brush.

Dab rise on cup with **Antique Mauve** and **Titanium White**. Tap suggestions of leaves with **Avocado**, **Blue Mist** and **Glazing Medium** using the tip of a #2 round brush.

Glaze a little **Antique Mauve** and **Glazing Medium** on the left edge of the cup and the saucer.

Napkin: Paint the edge of the napkin with a double loaded 1/2" angle shader with **Titanium White** and **Glazing Medium**. Shade with a little a little **Paynes Grey** and **Glazing Medium**. Paint a little row of dots on lace edge of the napkin with **Titanium White** and the tip of your liner brush.

Roses: **Titanium White** and **Antique Mauve**.

Squishy Leaves: Add a few more squish leaves as needed near the teacup. Paint pale stems on the right side of the cup.

Lettering: Paint lettering with **Raw Sienna** and **Glazing Medium** using 1/8" lettering brush. Edge letters on the right side with **Paynes Grey** using liner brush.

Ribbon: Paint ribbon with **Blue Mist** and **Glazing Medium**.

Tints: Glaze over background edges with **Glazing Medium** and **Blue Mist**. Glaze shadow under the edge of the saucer with **Paynes Gray**. Add touches of **Antique Mauve** in a few places under the roses.

1436 Lakeview Dr

THERMOMETER

°C
°F

LILACS
ADDRESS BOARD
PAGES 41, 46 - 47

GARDEN CLOCK
PAGES 48 - 49

WATERING CAN
THERMOMETER
PAGE 51

CONTAINER GARDENS
MEDIUM GOOSEBOARD
PAGES 50 - 53

GRAPES & VIBURNUM
WINE RACK
PAGES 60 - 63

Lilacs

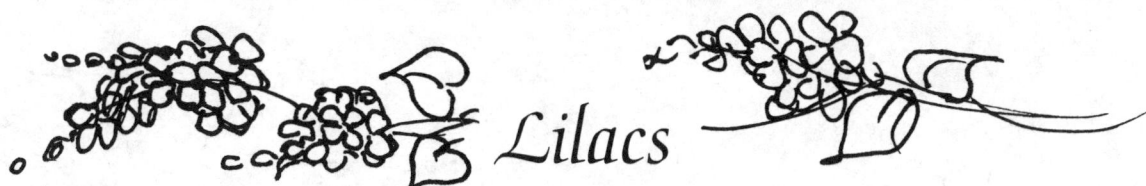

Surfaces: *Medium Routed Oval, Street Address Board (Stan Browns Arts & Crafts)*
Childs Tea Set

Paints: *DecoArt Americana Acrylics*

DA001 Titanium White	*DA052 Avocado*	*DA056 Olive Green*
DA064 Burnt Umber	*DA082 Evergreen*	*DA101 Dioxazine Purple*
DA141 Blue Violet	*DA152 Shale Green*	*DA158 Antique Teal*
DA178 Blue Mist	*DA153 Eggshell*	*DA068 Slate Grey*
Faux Glazing Medium		

Basecoat: *Routed Oval Board -* **JW White Lightning**. *Paint center area with* **Shale Green**, *accent route with* **Evergreen**
  Address Board - **Shale Green**, *insert -* **Eggshell**

Stems: *Paint stems in the glass container with various shades of green and Glazing Medium using the edge of your angle shader.*

Glass Container: *Paint edge of glass with a double loaded 1/2" angle shader. Touch the heel of the brush into glazing medium and brush the tip across the edge of* **Slate Grey**. *Brush down the edges and across the bottom. Highlight with* **Titanium White** *and accent with colors of the leaves and flowers.*

Leaves: *Paint squish leaves with lots of* **Glazing Medium** *with* **Avocado, Evergreen, Olive Green** *and* **Blue Mist**. *I used a #16 flat shader for the leaves in the vase of Lilacs and #12 and #8 for the leaves on the address board.*

Bow: **Blue Mist, Antique Teal, Titanium White** *and* **Faux Glazing Medium.**

Lilacs: **Dioxazine Purple, Titanium White, Titanium White** *and* **Faux Glazing Medium.**

Lettering: **Evergreen** *mixed with* **glazing medium.**

Finishing Touches: *Add a few more squishy leaves to nestle the flowers and add stems and squiqqles with* **Olive Green**.

Paint Lilacs nearest the bow first with the strongest colors. As you paint flowers toward the edge of your design, lighten the value by adding White and Glazing Medium.

Tea

Creamy Roses
Scissor Holder

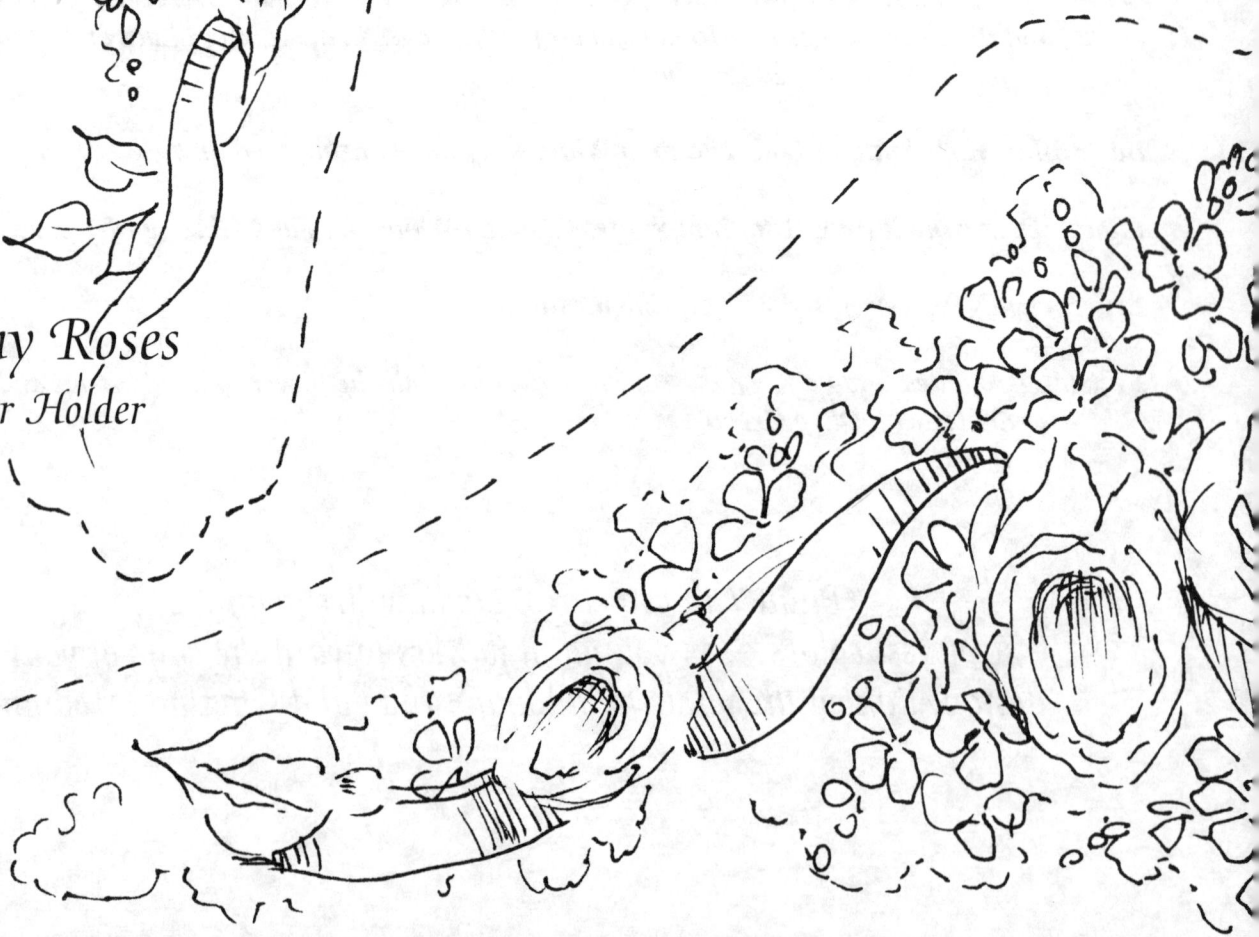

Time

Tea Time
Tea Box

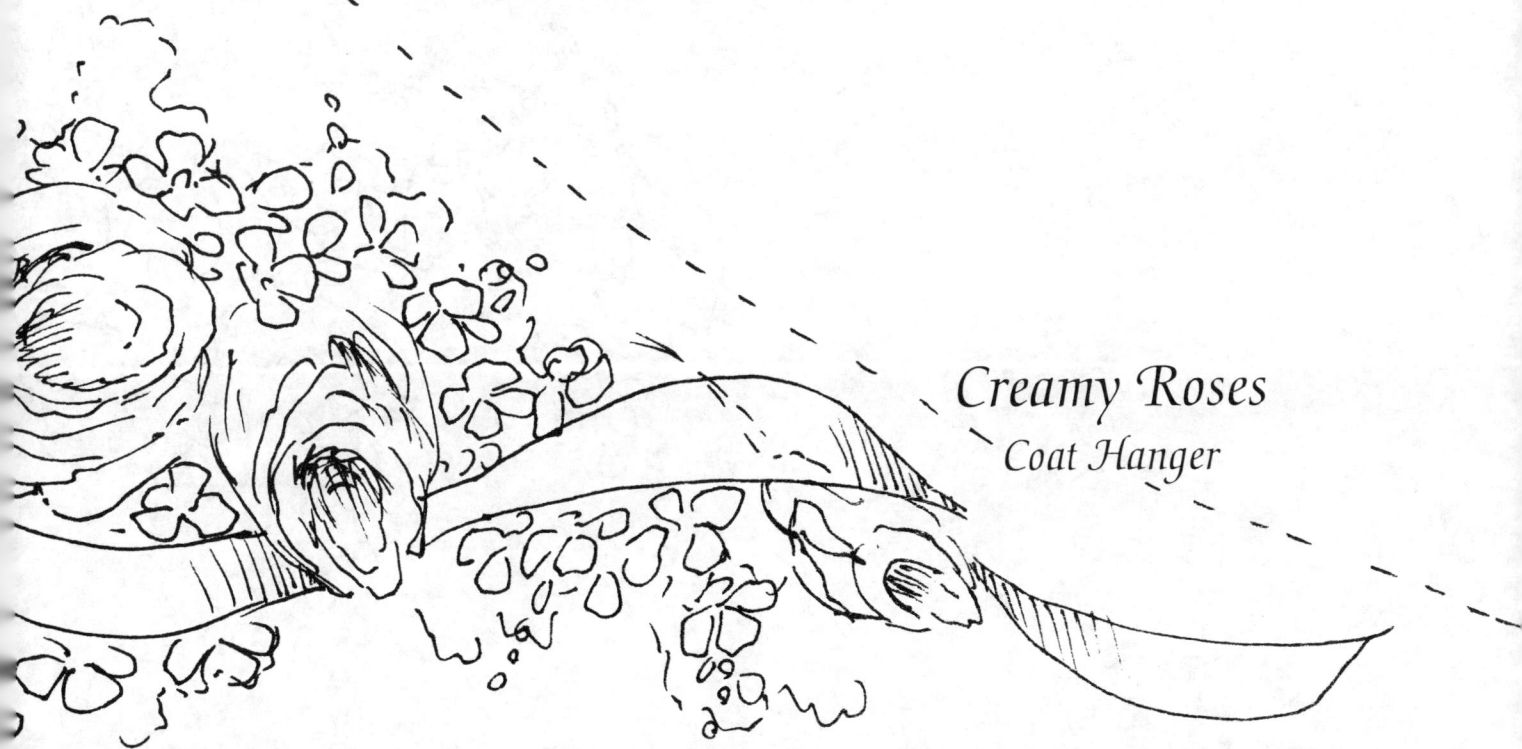

Creamy Roses
Coat Hanger

44

Lilacs
Medium Routed Oval

Lilacs
Street Address Board

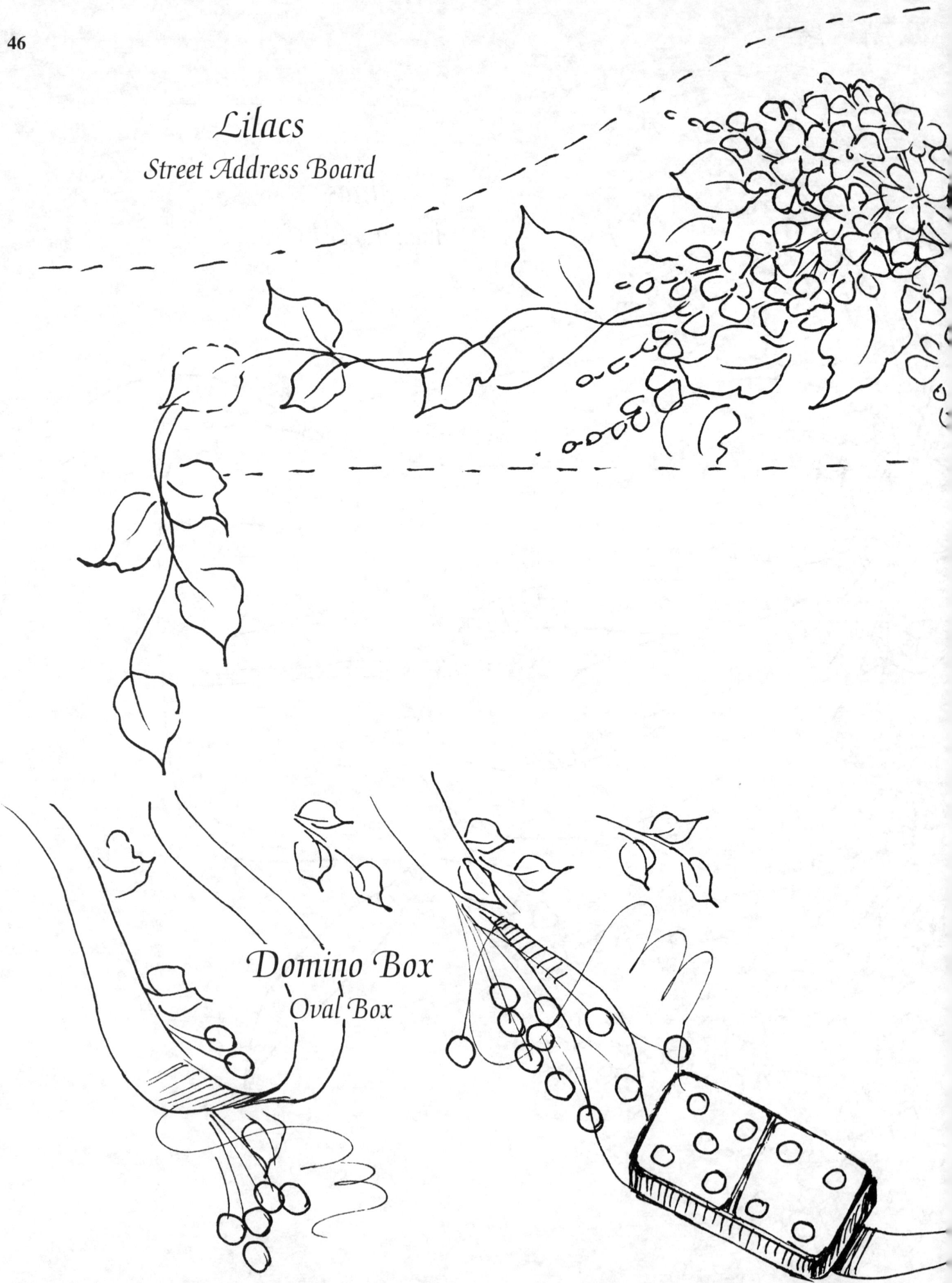

Domino Box
Oval Box

Domino Box

Surfaces: Oval Box

Palette: DecoArt Americana Acrylic

DA001 Titanium White	DA052 Avocado	DA056 Olive Green
DA064 Burnt Umber	DA082 Evergreen	DA093 Raw Sienna
DA101 Dioxazine Purple	DA152 Shale Green	DA141 Blue Violet
DA067 Lamp Black	DA158 Antique Teal	DA178 Blue Mist
Faux Glazing Medium		

48

Domino Box continued

Preparation: *Base coat with one coat of* **JW White Lightning**, *sand lightly. Tape stripe on side of box with 1/2" masking tape. Paint with a light coat of* **Glazing Medium** *and let dry. Paint stripes with* **Shale Green** *mixed with a little* **Glazing Medium**.

Pattern: *Trace and transfer dominos and lettering with gray graphite. Sand lightly.*

Branches: **Glazing Medium** *and* **Burnt Umber**.

Squishy Leaves: **Glazing Medium, Blue Mist, Evergreen** *and* **Avocado**.

Dominos: *Paint dominos with* **Lamp Black**. *Shade with a brush mix of* **Titanium White** *and* **Lamp Black**. *Add dots with* **Titanium White** *using the end of a paintbrush.*

Ribbon: **Blue Mist** *and* **Glazing Medium**. *Shade with* **Antique Teal** *and highlight with* **Titanium White**.

Berries: *Tap Berries with* **Dioxazine Purple, Blue Violet, Blue Mist, Glazing Medium** *and* **Titanium White** *using a Q-tip. Add stems with* **Burnt Umber** *or use .03 Brown Pigma Micron Pen.*

Squiggle: **Blue Mist**.

Lettering: **Shale Green**.

Background Tint: **Raw Sienna** *and* **Glazing Medium**.

Garden Clock

Surface: *Mantle Clock (Stan Brown's Arts & Crafts)*

Palette: Decoart Americana Acrylic

DA001 Titanium White	DA010 Cadmium Yellow	DA052 Avocado
DA056 Olive Green	DA063 Burnt Sienna	DA082 Evergreen
DA101 Dioxazine Purple	DA152 Shale Green	DA162 Antique Mauve
DA178 Blue Mist	DecoArt Americana Acrylic	Faux Glazing Medium

Basecoats: *Paint clock panel with* **Shale Green**. *Sand lightly.*

Foliage: *Tap foliage with* **Avocado, Evergreen, Blue Mist** *and* **Olive Green**. *Tap lower edge of foliage with* **Shale Green** *so that edge fades into background.*

Iris: **Dioxazine Purple**, *and* **Titanium White**.

Tulips: **Antique Mauve** *and* **Titanium White**.

Daisies: **Titanium White**.

49

Garden Clock continued
Center of Daisies: Cadmium Yellow shaded with Burnt Sienna and Cadmium Yellow.

Queen Ann's Lace: Olive Green, Avocado and Titanium White.

Grasses: Olive Green.

Filler Flowers: Dioxazine Purple and Titanium White.

Distant Delphinium: Dioxazine Purple and Glazing Medium.

Spatter: Titanium White.

Garden Clock
Mantle Clock

Container Gardens

Surfaces: Medium Goosecreek Signboard (Stan Brown's Arts & Crafts), Glass Jars

Palette: DecoArt Americana Acrylic

DA001 Titanium White	DA009 Antique Gold	DA010 Cadmium Yellow
DA011 Lemon Yellow	DA014 Cadmium Orange	DA052 Avocado
DA056 Olive Green	DA063 Burnt Sienna	DA064 Burnt Umber
DA079 Brandy Wine	DA082 Evergreen	DA093 Raw Sienna
DA101 Dioxazine Purple	DA141 Blue Violet	DA151 Royal Fuchsia
DA152 Shale Green	DA153 Eggshell	DA158 Antique Teal
DA167 Paynes Grey	DA178 Blue Mist	DA191 Camel
DA218 Gingerbread	Faux Glazing Medium	

Basecoats: Paint with one coat of **JW White Lightning**, sand lightly. Edge board with **Shale Green** mixed with **Glazing Medium** or color of choice.

Pattern: Trace and transfer containers using gray graphite.

Flower Pots: Paint flower pots with **Brandy Wine**. Highlight with **Gingerbread** using a double loaded 3/4" angle shader to fade in the edges. Shade pots with **Burnt Sienna**, **Burnt Umber**, **Dioxazine Purple** and **Glazing Medium**. Create rims by painting across the pot with double loaded brush with **Burnt Umber** in the tip and **Glazing Medium** in the heel of the brush.

Crock: Paint crock with **Eggshell**. Paint stripe with **Blue Violet** mixed with a little **Paynes Grey**. Shade with **Paynes Grey** and highlight with **Titanium White**.

Basket: Paint with **Burnt Umber**. Create weave of the basket with **Raw Sienna** and **Camel**.

Background Foliage: Tap foliage with **Avocado**, **Evergreen**, **Olive Green**, and **Blue Mist** using a 3/4" Foliage Brush.

Sunflowers: Paint sunflowers with **Antique Gold**, **Cadmium Yellow**, **Lemon Yellow**, **Burnt Umber**, **Burnt Sienna** and **Paynes Grey**.

Geranium: Paint geranium leaves with **Avocado** and highlight with **Olive Green** and **Blue Mist**. Shade to separate the leaves with **Evergreen**. Paint geraniums with **Cadmium Orange**, **Royal Fuchsia** and **Titanium White**.

Bow on Basket: Paint bow with **Blue Mist**. Shade with **Antique Teal** and highlight with **Titanium White**.

Daisies: Paint daisy petals and centers with **Titanium White**. Paint centers with **Cadmium Yellow** and shade with **Raw Sienna**.

Filler Flowers: Paint filler flowers with **Dioxazine Purple**, **Blue Violet** and **Titanium White**.

Ferns: Tap ferns with **Avocado**, **Evergreen**, **Olive Green**, **Blue Mist**, and **Glazing Medium**.

Finishing Touches: Shade under containers with a double loaded 3/4" angle shader with **Burnt Umber** and **Paynes Grey** in the point and **Glazing Medium** in the heel.

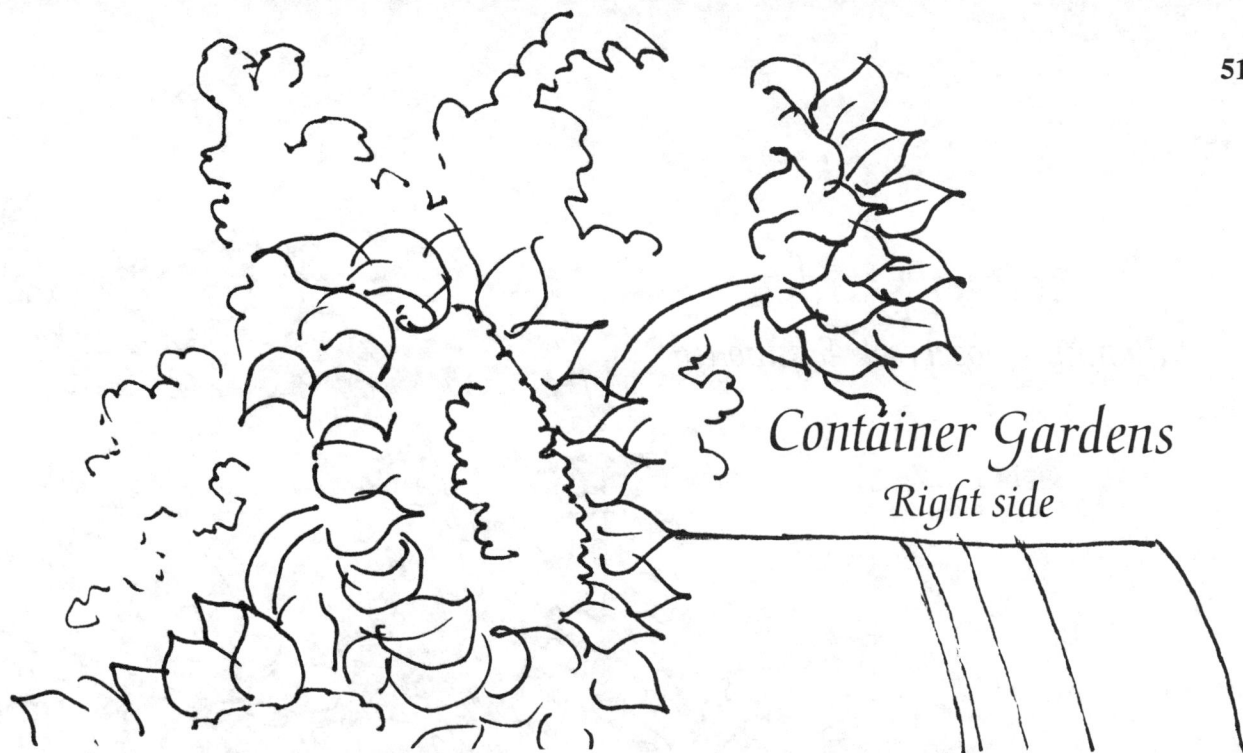

Container Gardens
Right side

Watering Can Thermometer

Surface: Thermometer (Stan Brown's Arts and Crafts)

Palette: DecoArt Americana Acrylic

DA001 Titanium White	DA052 Avocado	DA056 Olive Green
DA082 Evergreen	DA093 Raw Sienna	DA167 Paynes Grey
DA068 Slate Grey	DA063 Burnt Sienna	DA152 Shale Green
DA178 Blue Mist	Faux Glazing Medium	

Preparation: Paint wood surface with **J W White Lightning**. Sand lightly. Mask stripes with 1/2" masking tape. Paint with light coat of **Faux Glazing Medium** and let dry. Paint stripes with **Shale Green** mixed with **Faux Glazing Medium**.

Vines and Squishy Leaves: **Faux Glazing Medium, Avocado, Evergreen, Blue Mist** and **Olive Green**.

Watering Can: Base with **Slate Grey**. Shade with **Paynes Grey** and **Faux Glazing Medium**. Highlight using a double loaded brush with **Titanium White** and **Paynes Grey**. Wet the surface of the can with water and while still wet, touch dots of **Burnt Sienna** with the tip of a liner brush. Rust spots will bleed on the the damp surface.

Spatter: Spatter with **Paynes Grey** mixed with water.

Container Gardens
Medium Goosecreek Signboard

Geranium

Geranium Basket
Oval Hanging Sign

*Place this outside your front door
and add a few pots of Geraniums
for just the right touch.*

Geranium Basket

Surfaces: *Oval Hanging Sign (Steph's Folk Art Studio)*

Paints: DecoArt Americana Acrylic

DA001 Titanium White	DA014 Cadmium Orange	DA052 Avocado
DA056 Olive Green	DA064 Burnt Umber	DA082 Evergreen
DA093 Raw Sienna	DA148 Emperor's Gold	DA151 Royal Fuchsia
DA171 Driftwood	DA178 Blue Mist	DA191 Camel
Faux Glazing Medium		

Basecoats: Paint with **Driftwood** or color of choice, sand lightly.

Pattern: Trace and transfer the shape of the basket and Lettering.

Basket: Base with **Burnt Umber.** Paint weave of the basket with **Raw Sienna** and **Camel.**

Geranium Leaves: **Avocado, Evergreen, Olive Green,** and **Blue Mist** using a 1/2" Oval Wash Brush.

Geraniums: **Cadmium Orange, Royal Fuchsia** and **Titanium White**

Lettering: **Emperor's Gold.**

Touch O' Red

Surfaces: *Assorted white with red rim enamelware.*
It is fun to collect this neat stuff and the more beat up the better.

Palette: DecoArt Americana Acrylic

DA001 Titanium White	DA014 Cadmium Orange	DA019 Berry Red
DA052 Avocado	DA056 Olive Green	DA064 Burnt Umber
DA082 Evergreen	DA101 Dioxazine Purple	DA165 Napa Red
DA178 Blue Mist	Faux Glazing Medium	

Preparation: Wash in hot soapy water. Spray new tinware lightly with **Krylon Matte Spray** or paint with **DecoArt Multipurpose Sealer.**

Pattern: Trace and transfer fruits as needed with gray graphite.

Note: Directions and diagrams in the front of the book and the colors are listed here for reference.

Leaves: **Avocado, Olive Green, Blue Mist** and **Evergreen.**

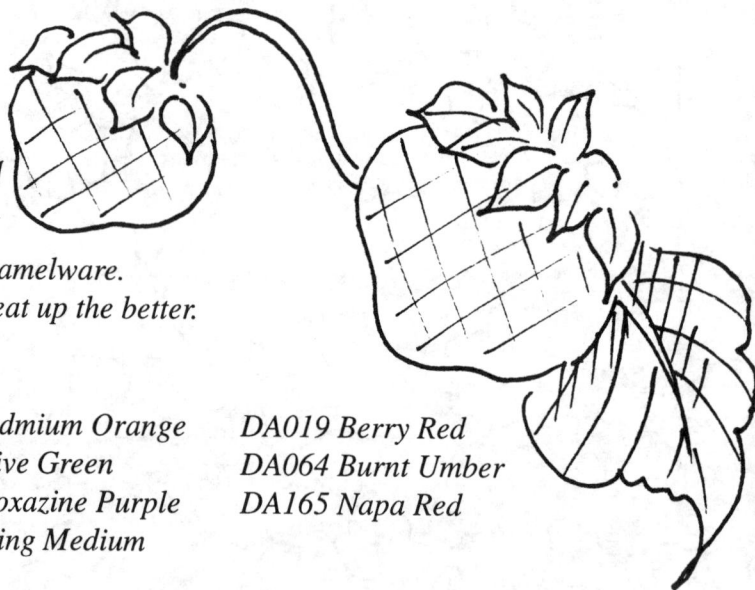

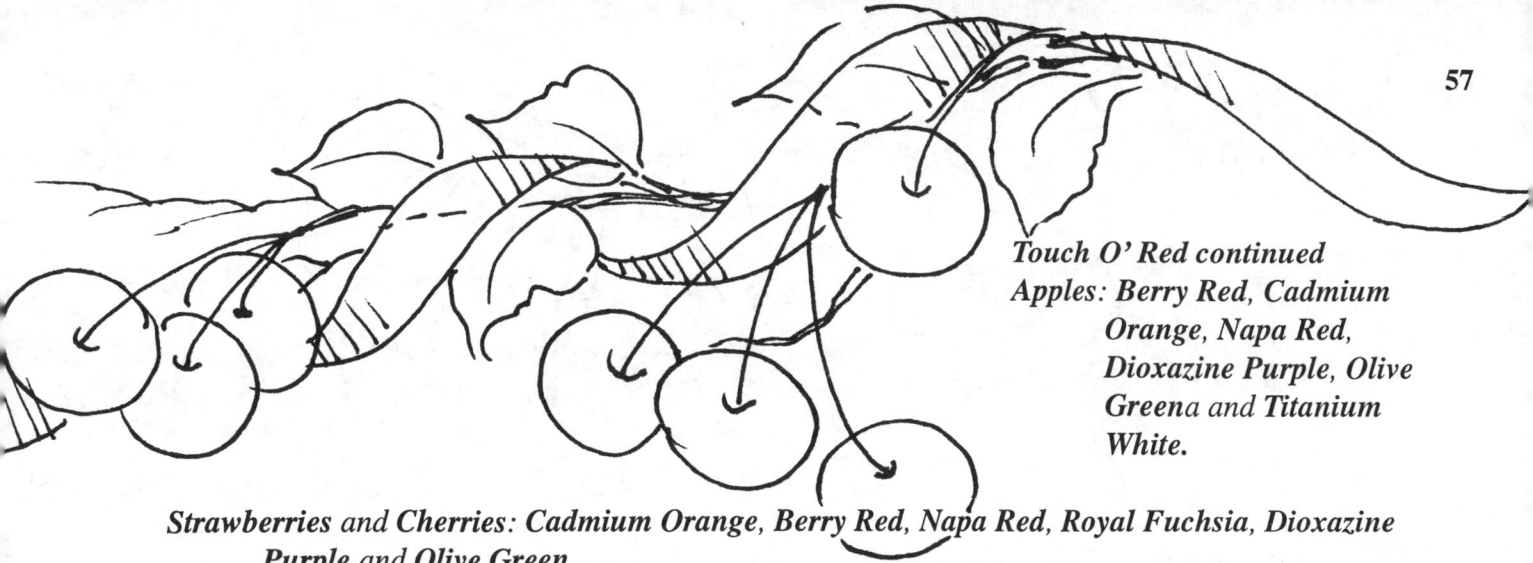

Touch O' Red continued
Apples: *Berry Red, Cadmium Orange, Napa Red, Dioxazine Purple, Olive Green*a *and Titanium White.*

Strawberries *and* **Cherries:** *Cadmium Orange, Berry Red, Napa Red, Royal Fuchsia, Dioxazine Purple and Olive Green.*

Geranium Leaves: *Avocado, Evergreen, Olive Green, and Blue Mist using a 1/2" Oval Wash Brush.*

Geraniums: *Cadmium Orange, Royal Fuchsia and Titanium White*

Finishing Touches: *Paint branches with* **Burnt Umber.** *Paints stems and squiggles with* **Avocado,** *or Olive* **Green.** *Spatter as desired.*

Touch O' Red
Black Tin Plate

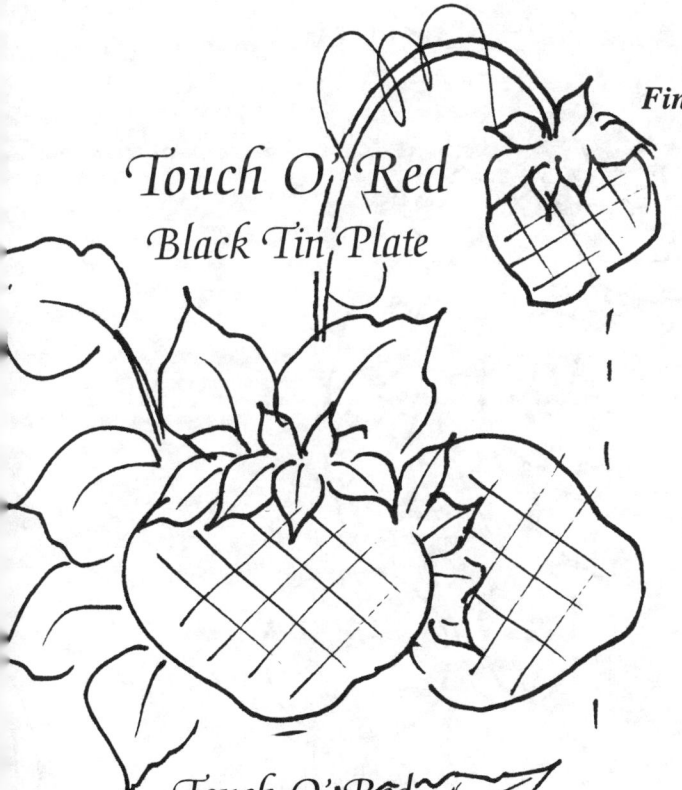

Touch O' Red
Geranium Enamel Box

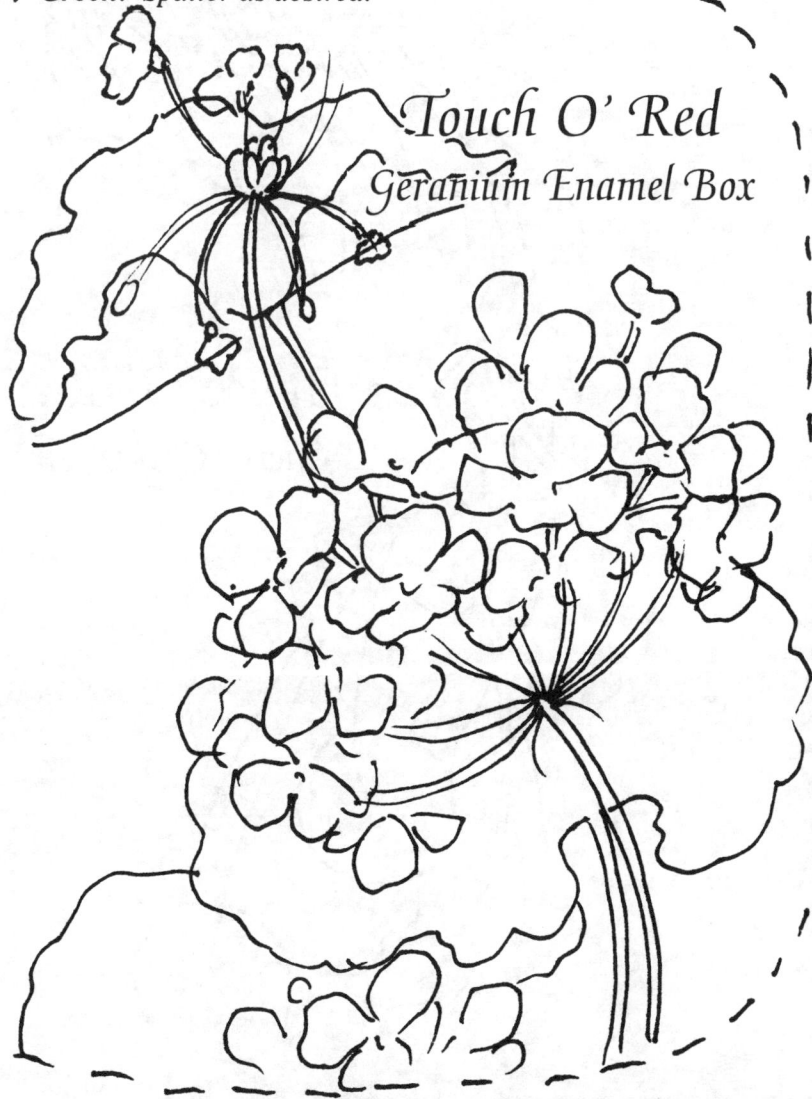

Touch O' Red
Black Tin Box

Touch O' Red
Cherry Enamel Bowl & Jar

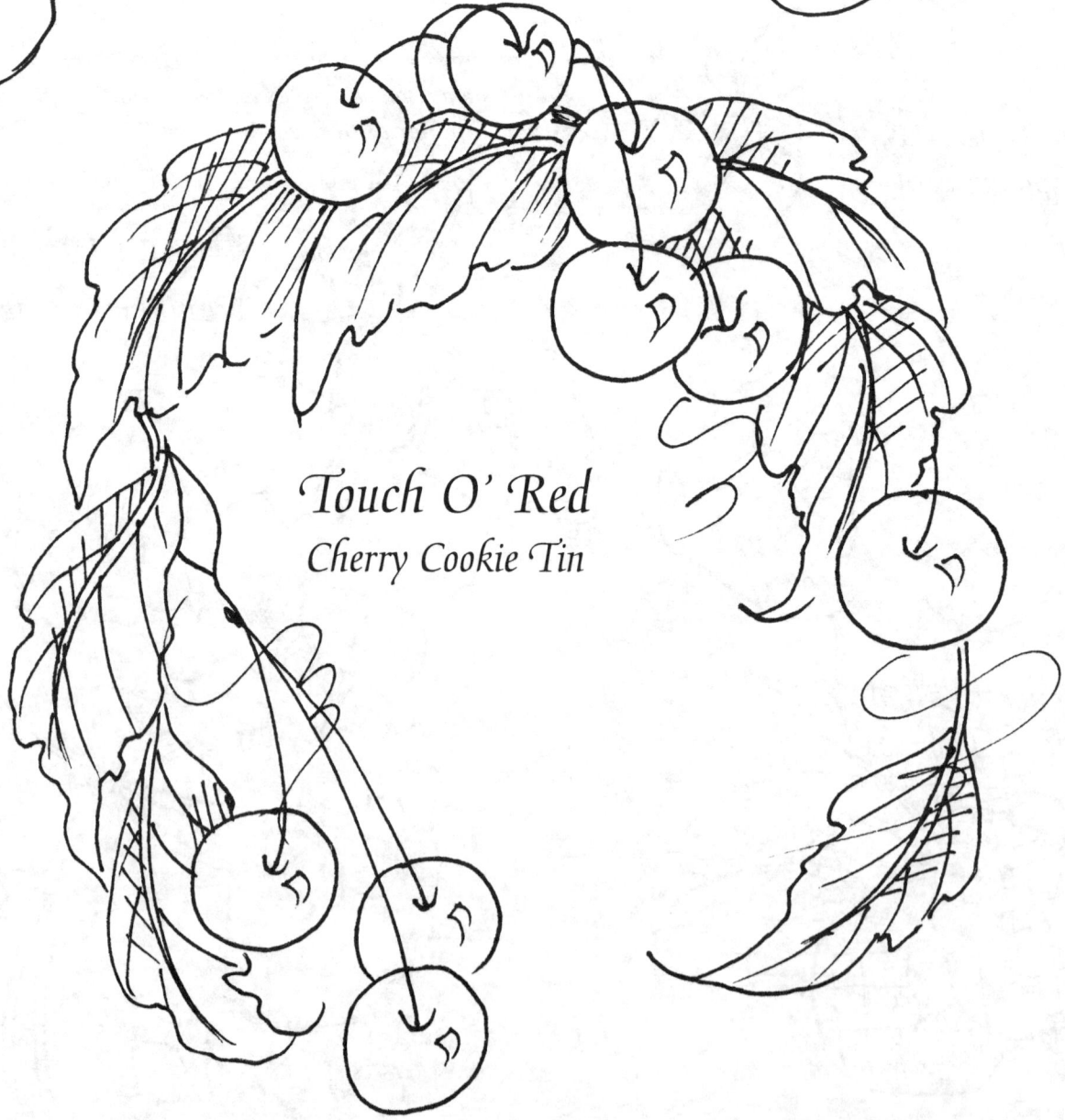

Touch O' Red
Cherry Cookie Tin

© 2001
Ros

Touch O' Red
Apple Enamel Bowl

Grapes and Viburnum

Surfaces: Wine Rack (Stan Brown's Arts and
Crafts), Mini Oval Box

Palette: DecoArt Americana Acrylic
DA001 Titanium White
DA011 Lemon Yellow
DA052 Avocado
DA056 Olive Green
DA064 Burnt Umber
DA082 Evergreen
DA101 Dioxazine Purple
DA158 Antique Teal
DA167 Paynes Grey
DA178 Blue Mist
DA197 Violet Haze
Faux Glazing Medium

Preparation: Paint with
one coat of **JW**
White Lightning
and sand lightly.

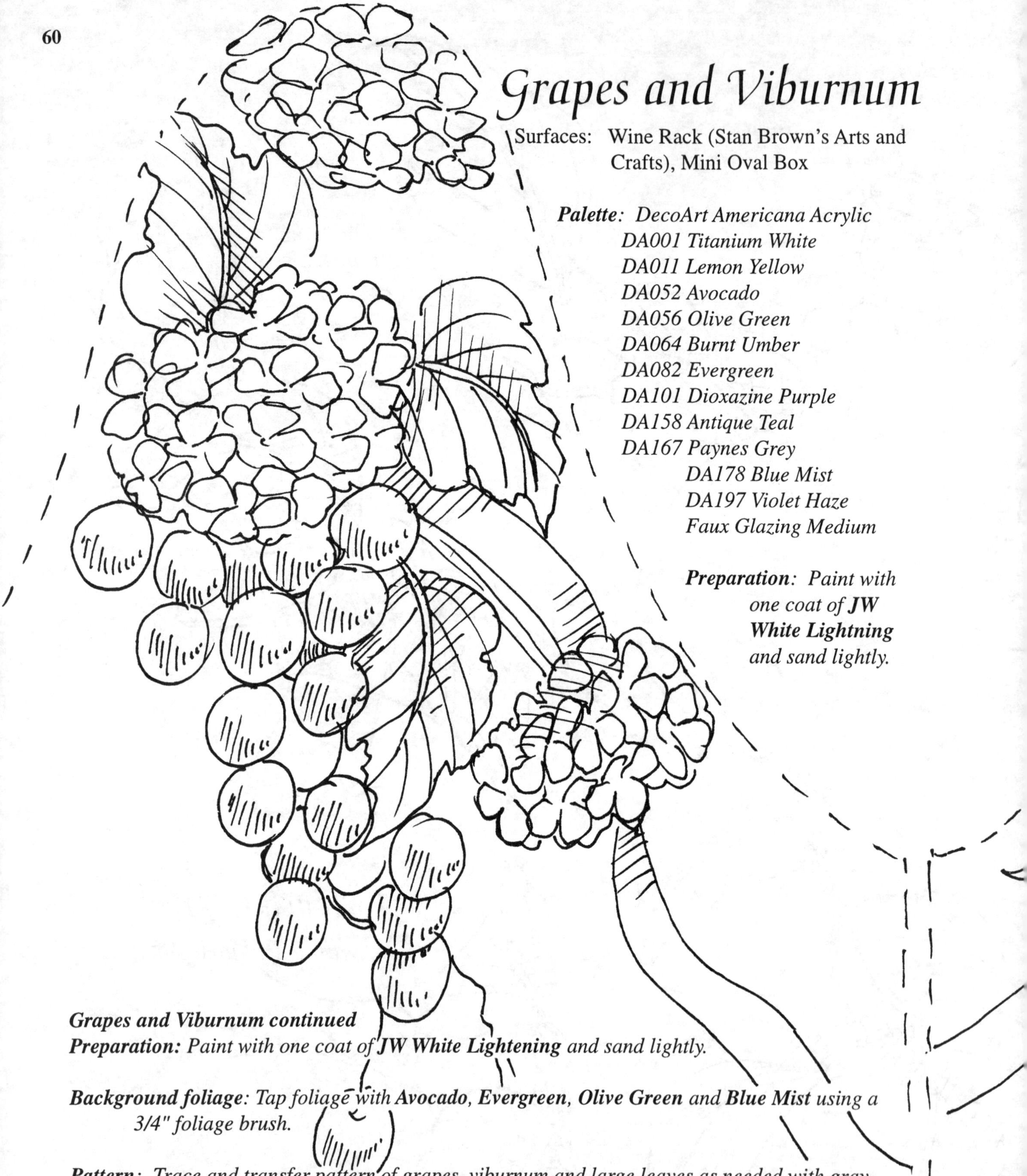

Grapes and Viburnum continued
Preparation: *Paint with one coat of **JW White Lightening** and sand lightly.*

Background foliage: *Tap foliage with **Avocado**, **Evergreen**, **Olive Green** and **Blue Mist** using a 3/4" foliage brush.*

Pattern: *Trace and transfer pattern of grapes, viburnum and large leaves as needed with gray graphite.*

Grapes: *Base grapes with **Olive Green**. Shade with **Blue Mist** and **Evergreen**. Highlight with **Lemon Yellow** and **Titanium White**. Accent with **Dioxazine Purple**, **Antique Teal** and **Violet Haze**.*

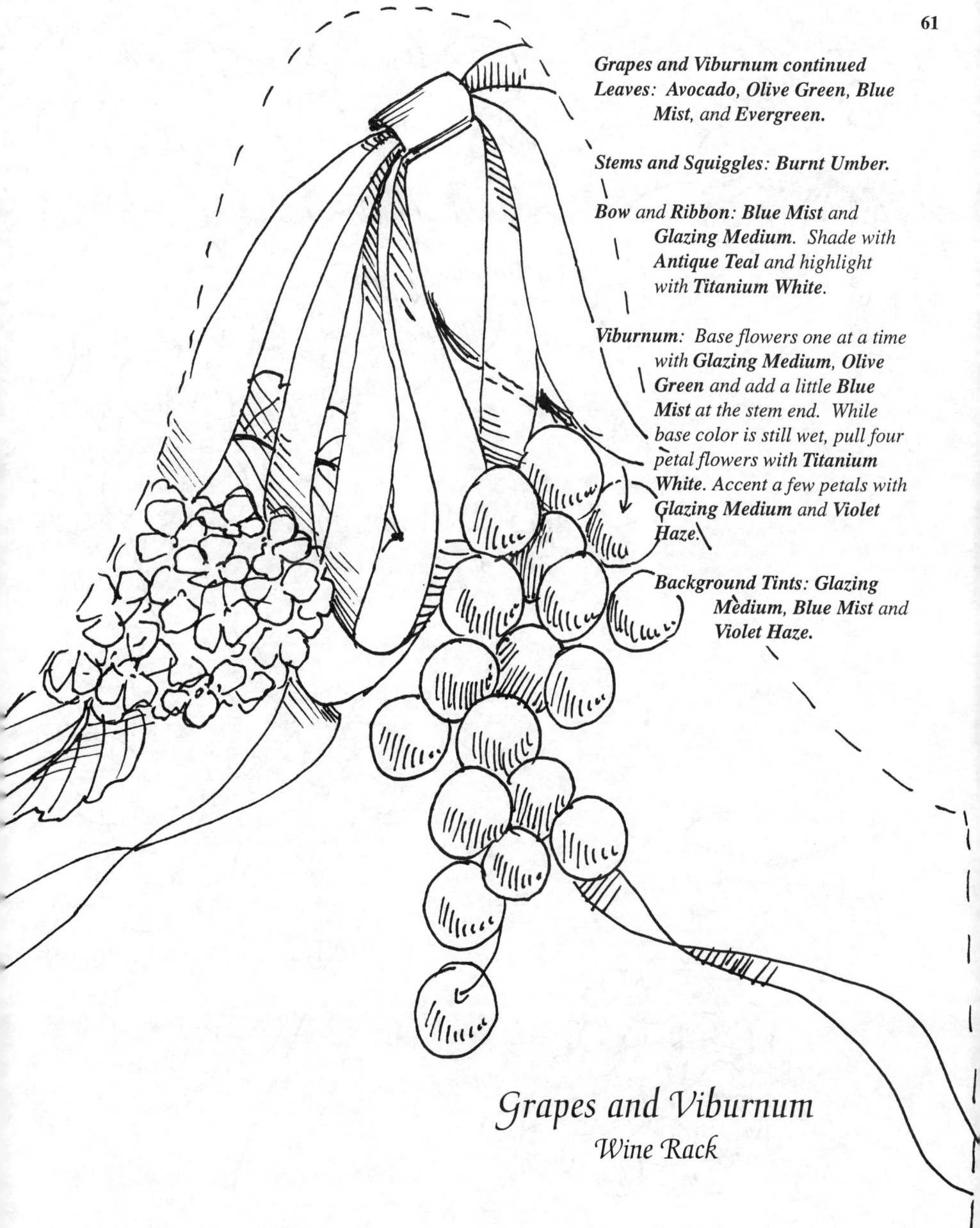

Grapes and Viburnum continued
Leaves: *Avocado, Olive Green, Blue Mist,* and *Evergreen.*

Stems and Squiggles: *Burnt Umber.*

Bow and **Ribbon:** *Blue Mist* and *Glazing Medium.* Shade with *Antique Teal* and highlight with *Titanium White.*

Viburnum: Base flowers one at a time with *Glazing Medium, Olive Green* and add a little *Blue Mist* at the stem end. While base color is still wet, pull four petal flowers with *Titanium White.* Accent a few petals with *Glazing Medium* and *Violet Haze.*

Background Tints: *Glazing Medium, Blue Mist* and *Violet Haze.*

Grapes and Viburnum
Wine Rack

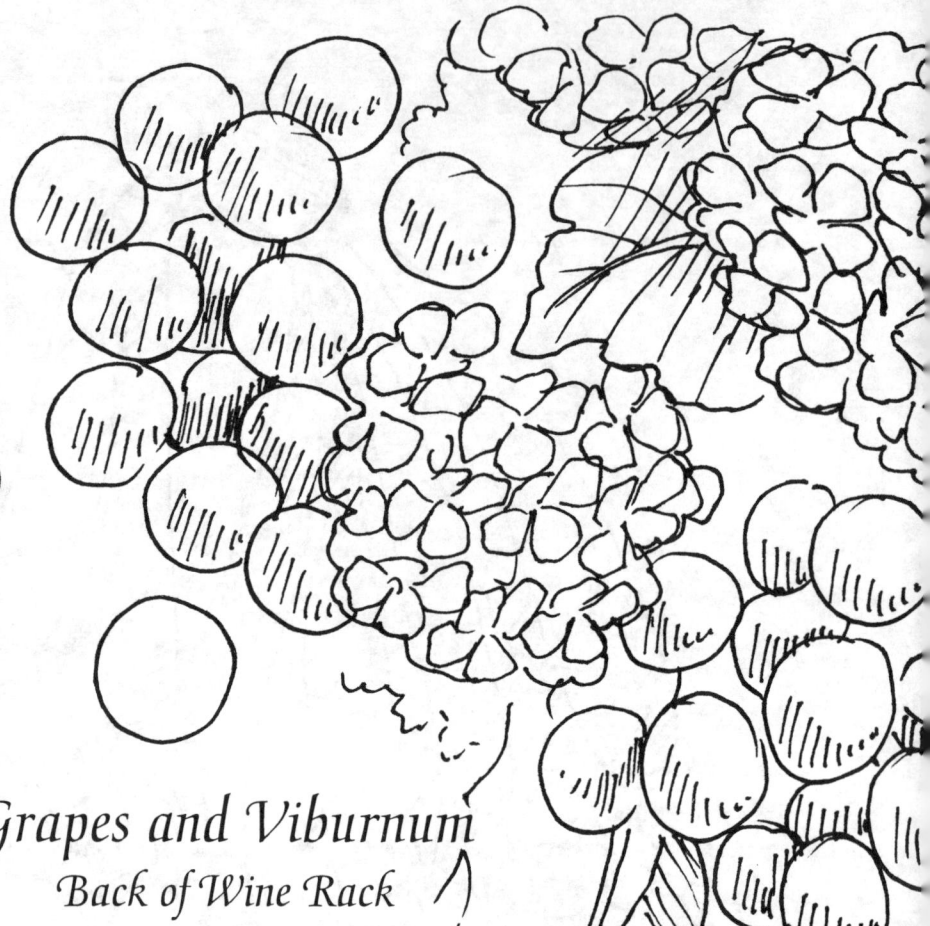

Grapes and Viburnum
Back of Wine Rack

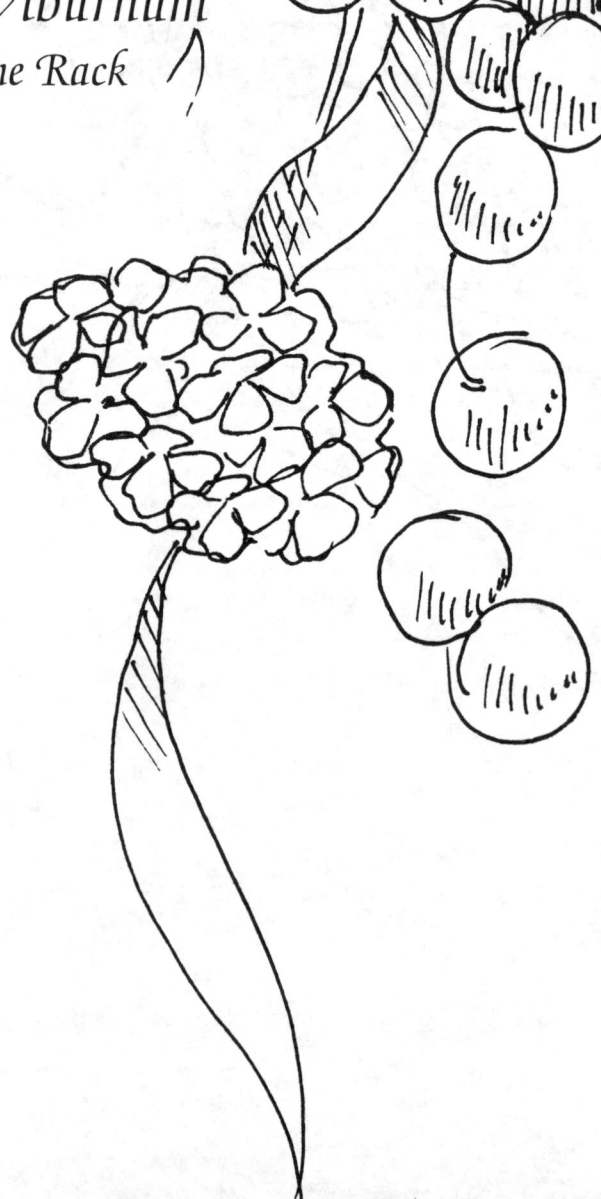

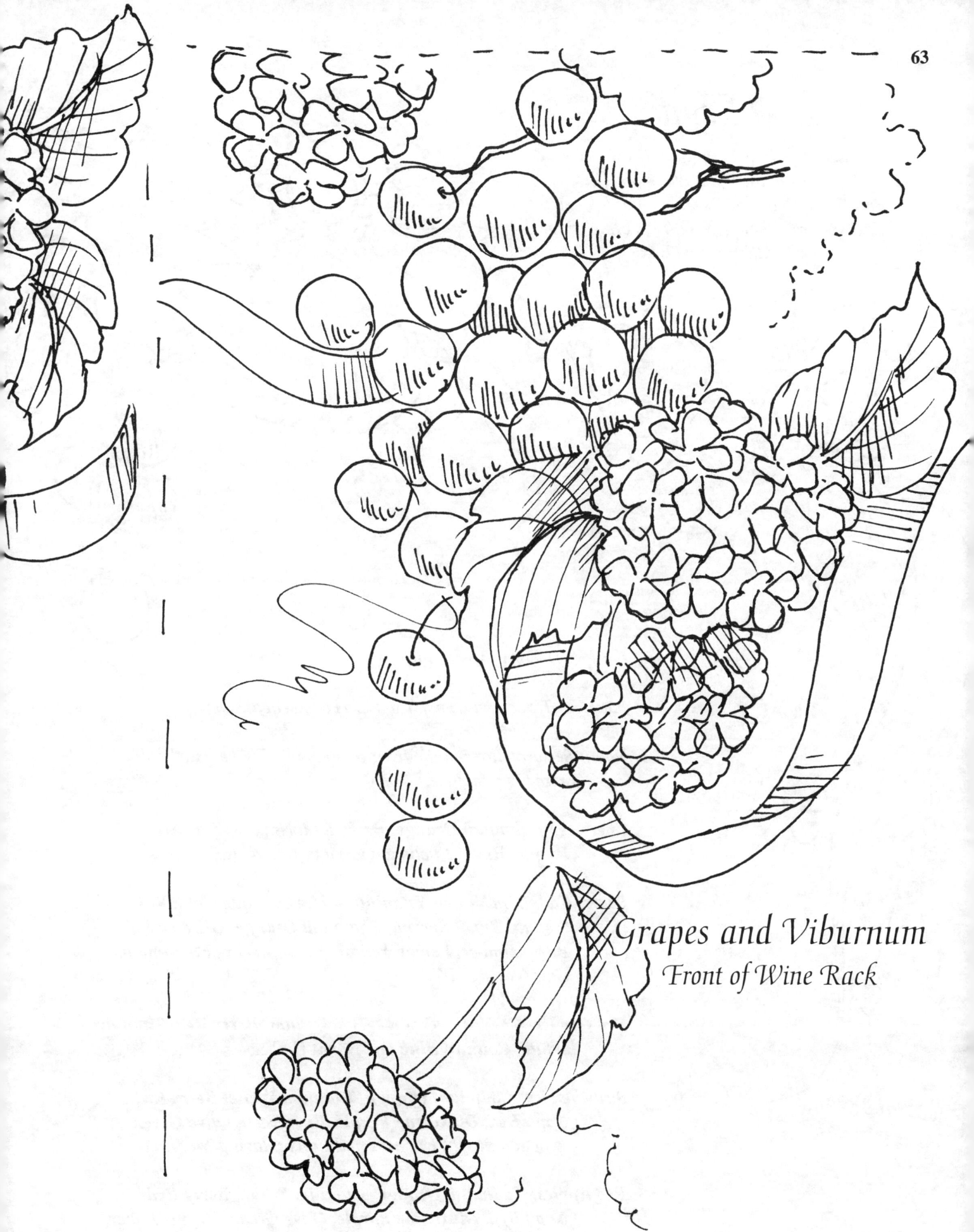

Grapes and Viburnum
Front of Wine Rack

Fruit

Surface: *Du Jour Sign (Stan Brown's Arts & Crafts), Large Railroad Lunchbox (Painter's Paradise), Red Grapes Chalkboard, Cherries Chalkboard, Cherry Wood Tray (Tolebridge), Cherry Tote Box*

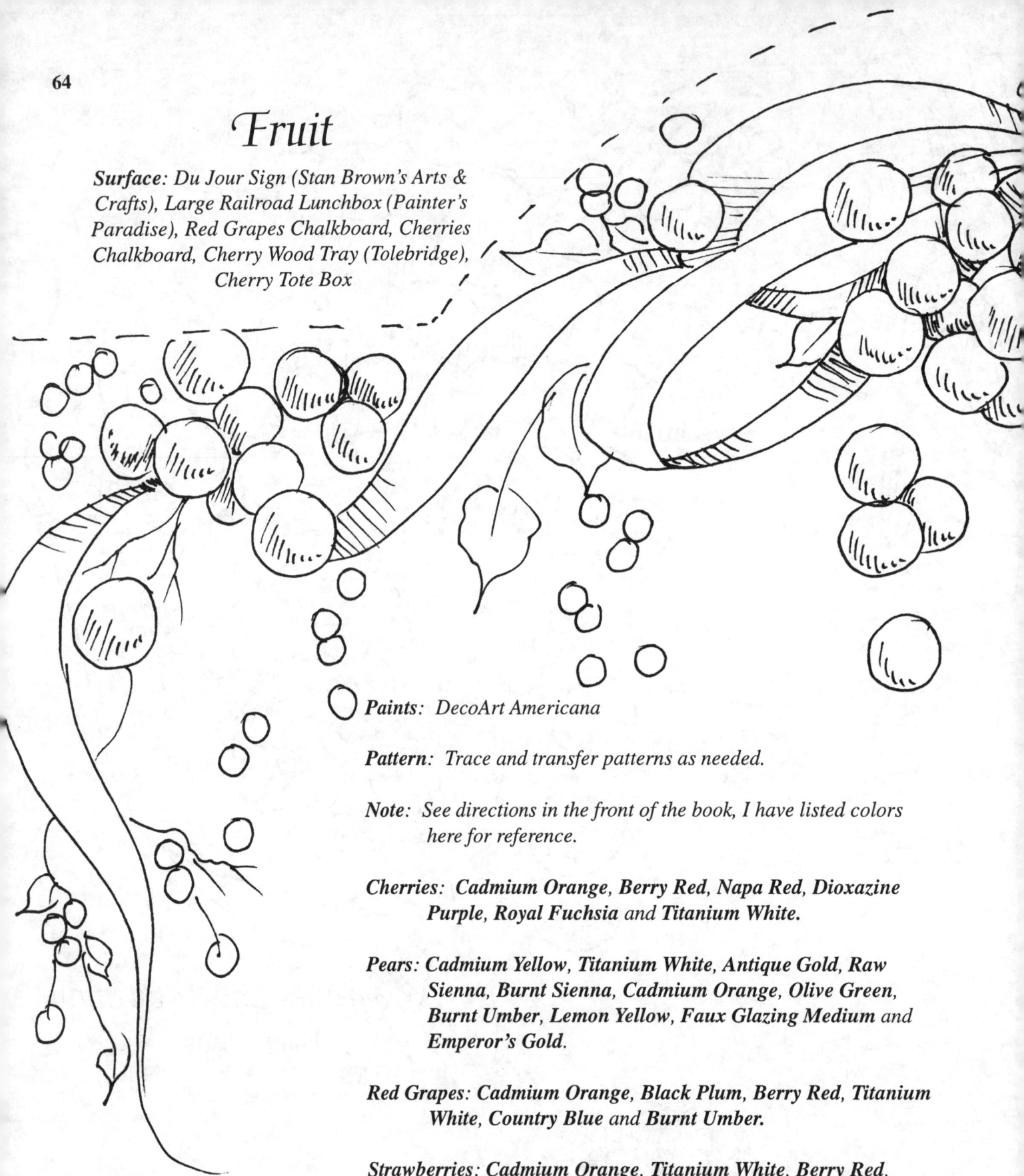

Paints: *DecoArt Americana*

Pattern: *Trace and transfer patterns as needed.*

Note: *See directions in the front of the book, I have listed colors here for reference.*

Cherries: *Cadmium Orange, Berry Red, Napa Red, Dioxazine Purple, Royal Fuchsia and Titanium White.*

Pears: *Cadmium Yellow, Titanium White, Antique Gold, Raw Sienna, Burnt Sienna, Cadmium Orange, Olive Green, Burnt Umber, Lemon Yellow, Faux Glazing Medium and Emperor's Gold.*

Red Grapes: *Cadmium Orange, Black Plum, Berry Red, Titanium White, Country Blue and Burnt Umber.*

Strawberries: *Cadmium Orange, Titanium White, Berry Red, Napa Red, Dioxazine Purple, Evergreen, Olive Green, Avocado, Royal Fuchsia and Faux Glazing Medium.*

Red Apples: *Cadmium Orange, Titanium White, Berry Red, Napa Red, Dioxazine Purple, Olive Green, Burnt Umber, Faux Glazing Medium, and Emperor's Gold.*

Geraniums

GERANIUMS
PAGES 54 - 56

FRUIT
RED GRAPES CHALKBOARD
RAILROAD LUNCH BOX
DU JOUR SIGN
PAGES 64 - 69, 72 - 73

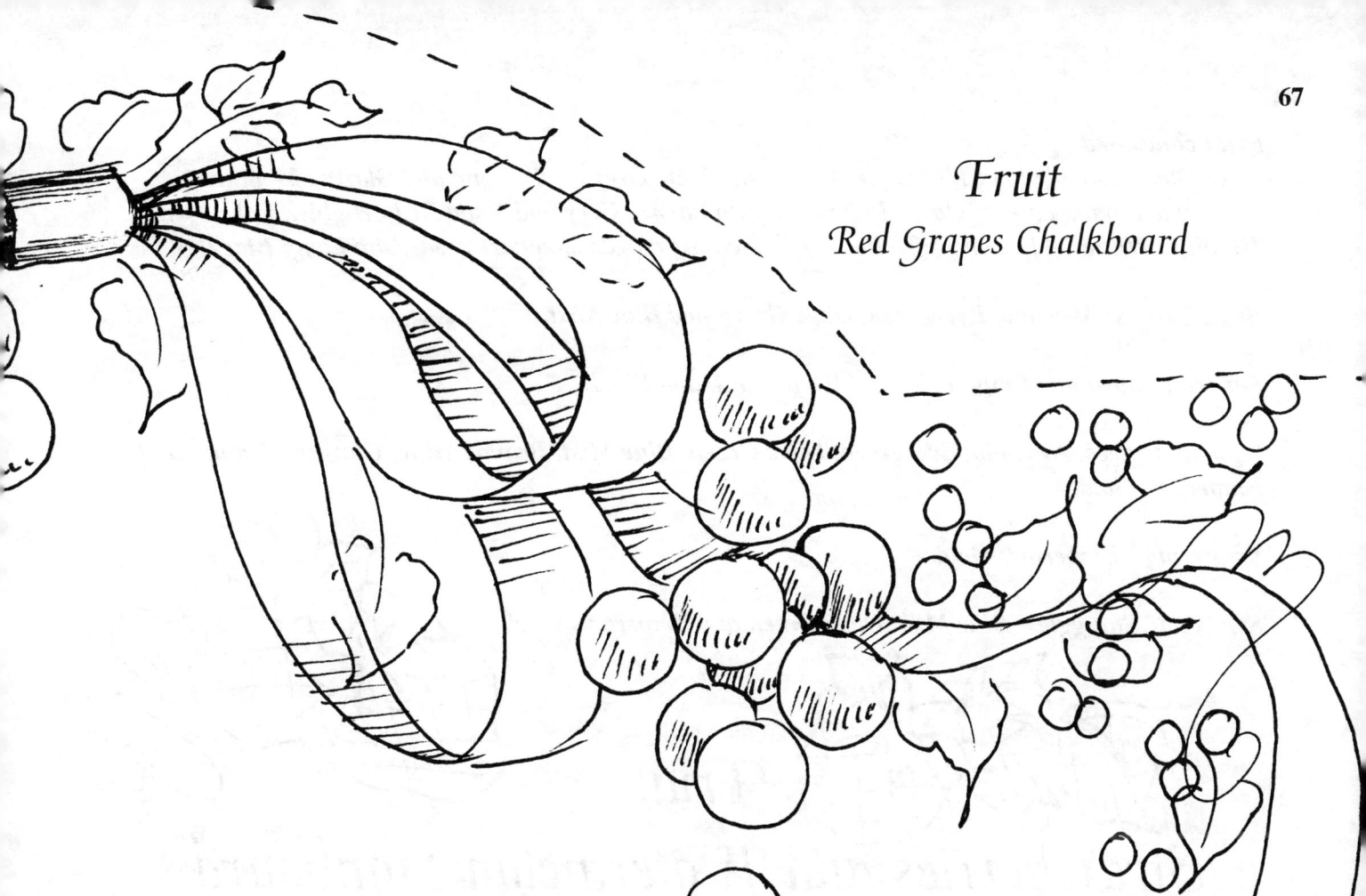

Fruit continued

Apple Slices: Base with **Buttermilk**, Shade with **Raw Sienna**, adds touches of **Olive Green**. Paint Seeds and Stem with **Burnt Umber** and highlight with **Buttermilk**. Edge with apple colors.

Green Apples: Olive Green, Titanium White, Blue Mist, Evergreen, Lemon Yellow, Cadmium Orange, Faux Glazing Medium and Emperor's Gold.

Golden Delicious: Cadmium Yellow, Titanium White, Antique Gold, Raw Sienna, Burnt Sienna, Cadmium Orange, Olive Green, Burnt Umber, Lemon Yellow, Faux Glazing Medium and Emperor's Gold.

Royal Gala: Cadmium Yellow, Cadmium Orange, Titanium White, Berry Red, Napa Red, Dioxazine Purple, Olive Green, Burnt Umber, Faux Glazing Medium and Emperor's Gold.

Raspberries: Black Plum, Dioxazine Purple, Napa Red, Titanium White, Olive Green, Glazing Medium and Emperor's Gold.

Berries: Cadmium Orange, Black Plum, Titanium White, Napa Red, Blue Mist, Glazing Medium and Emperor's Gold.

Fruit continued

Wine Glass: *Double load 1/2" angle shader with* **Slate Grey** *on the point and* **Glazing Medium** *in the heel and paint edge of glass. Paint wine with* **Paynes Grey** *and* **Napa Red**. *Highlight glass with* **Titanium White**. *Add some reflections of fruit colors and deepen dark areas with* **Lamp Black**.

Basic Leaves: *Avocado, Evergreen, Olive Green and Blue Mist.*

Lettering: *du Jour -* **Emperor's Gold** *lined with* **Lamp Black**.

Squishy Leaves: *Avocado, Evergreen, Olive Green, Blue Mist, Brandy Wine, Glazing Medium and Emperor's Gold.*

Spattering: *Emperor's Gold.*

Stems *and* **Squiggles:** *Blue Mist, Olive Green and Emperor's Gold.*

Fruit
Strawberries and Watermelon Signboard

(Stan Brown's Arts and Crafts)

I hate to sit and watch paint dry so I hop around while painting fruit. While one thing is drying paint another area of your painting.

Ribbons and Bows: *Paint with color of choice. Practice first on a piece of acetate and lay on your surface to see if you like the color. Mix a puddle of color and glazing medium and paint ribbon strokes with 1/2" angle shader.*

Basket: *Burnt Umber, Raw Sienna, Camel*

Chalkboard: *Any old piece of wood or masonite can be turned into a chalkboard. Paint with Crayola (Benjamin Moore) Chalkboard Paint.*

*Prop this signboard on an easel for a great
little "menu board".*

Du Jour

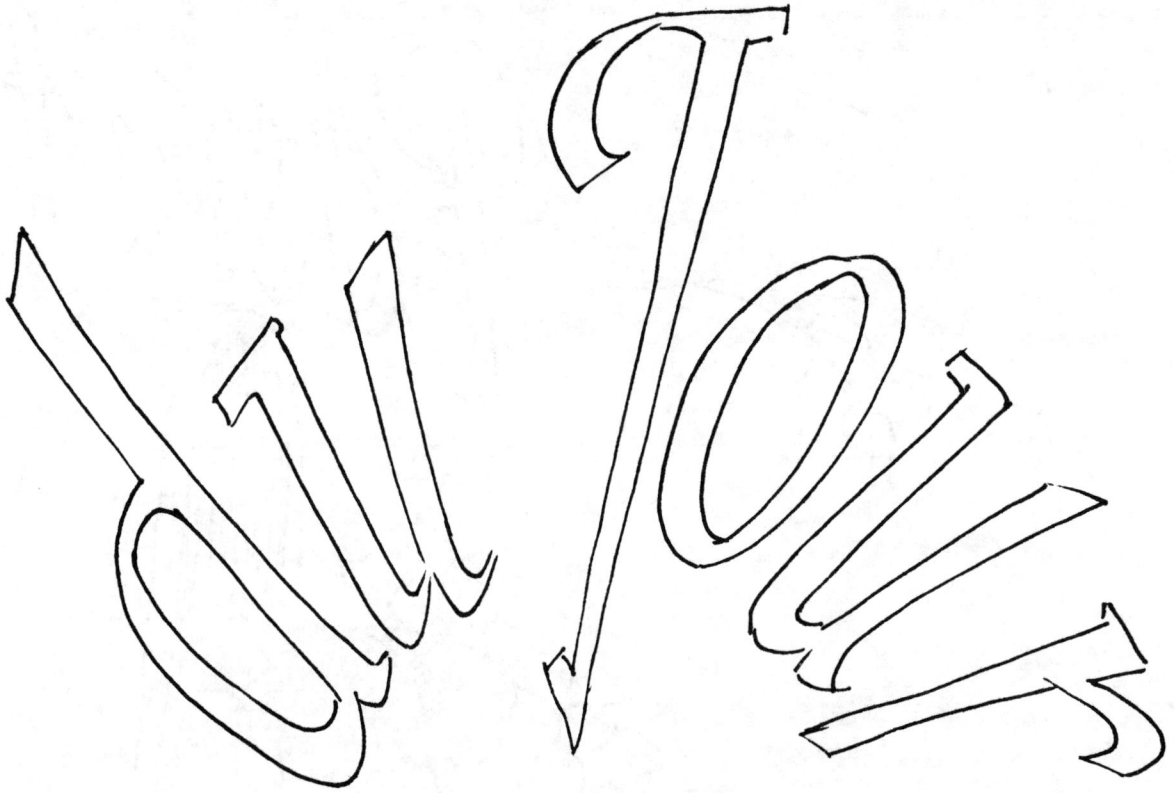

Fruit
Du Jour Sign

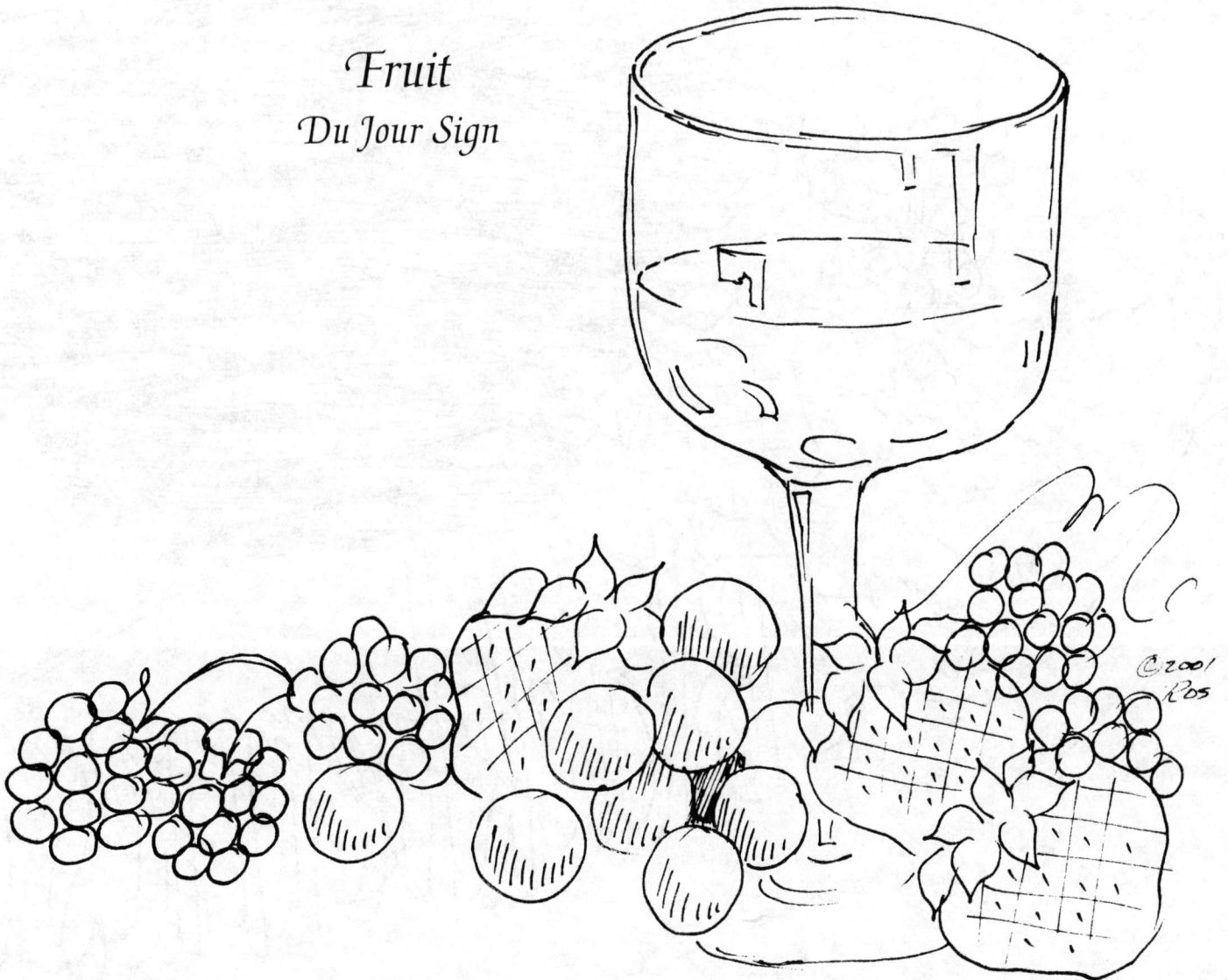

©2001
Ros

Basket of Blackberries &

Strawberries

Fruit
Strawberries & Watermelon Signboard

Watermelon

72

Fruit
Large Railroad Lunchbox

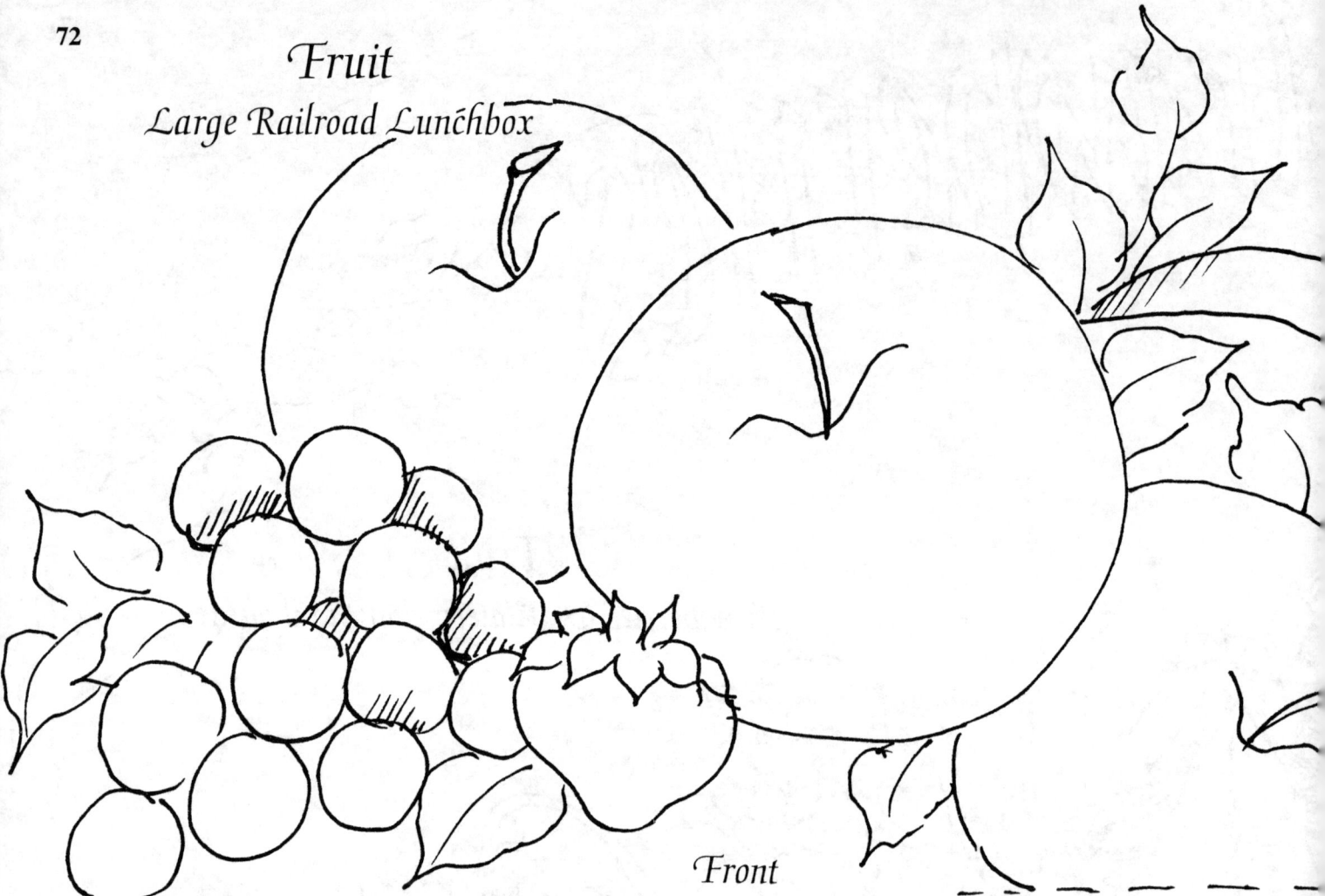

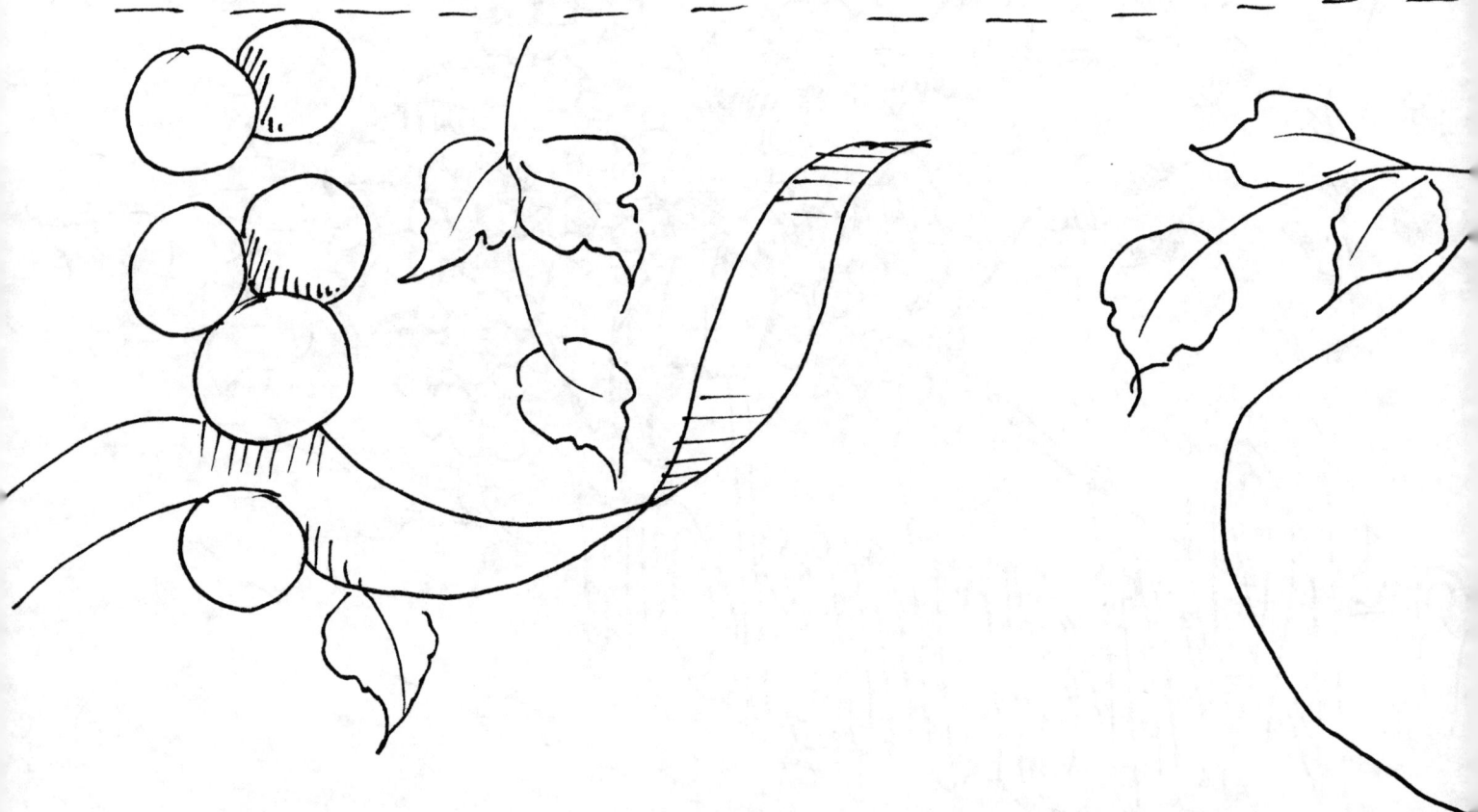

Front

Side

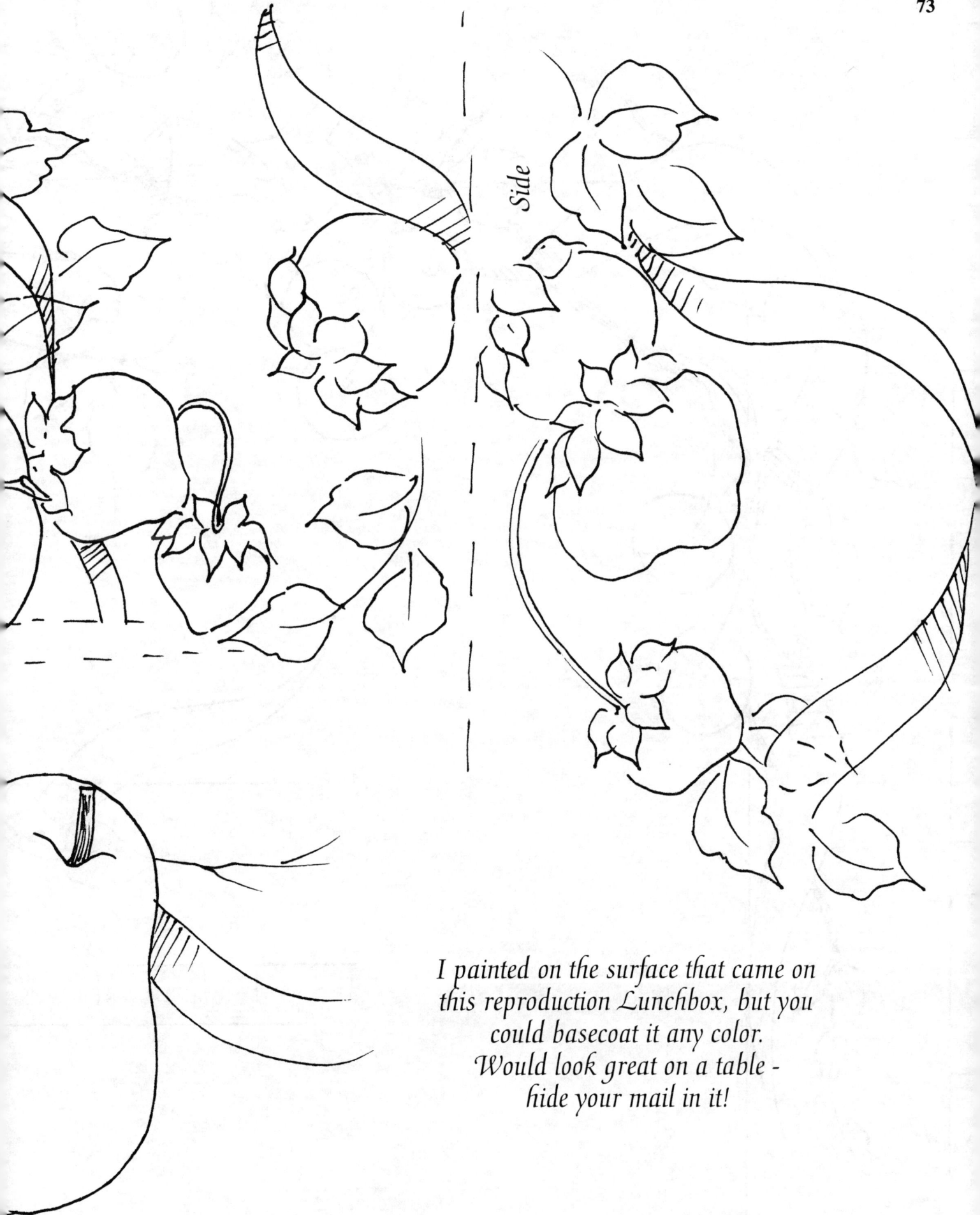

I painted on the surface that came on this reproduction Lunchbox, but you could basecoat it any color. Would look great on a table - hide your mail in it!

TOUCH O' RED
ENAMELWARE LADLE
JAR
PAGES 56 - 58

FRUIT
CHERRY WOOD TRAY
CHERRY TOTE BOX
PAGES 64 - 67, 78 - 81

Cherries

Cadmium Orange

Royal Fuchsia

Berry Red

Napa Red

Diox. Purple

Base with
Cadmium Orange

Shade with
Royal Fuchsia &
Napa Red.

Highlight with
Cadmium Orange &
White

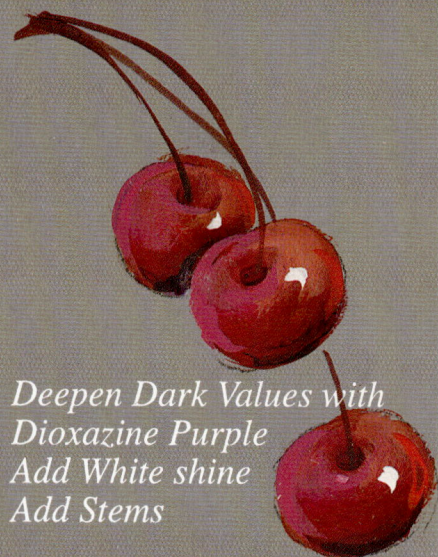

Deepen Dark Values with
Dioxazine Purple
Add White shine
Add Stems

Green Grapes

Titanium White

Olive Green

Blue Mist

Evergreen

Pineapple

Lemon

Violet Haze

Base Grapes with
Olive Green

Shade with
Blue Mist &
Evergreen

Highlight with
Lemon &
Pineapple

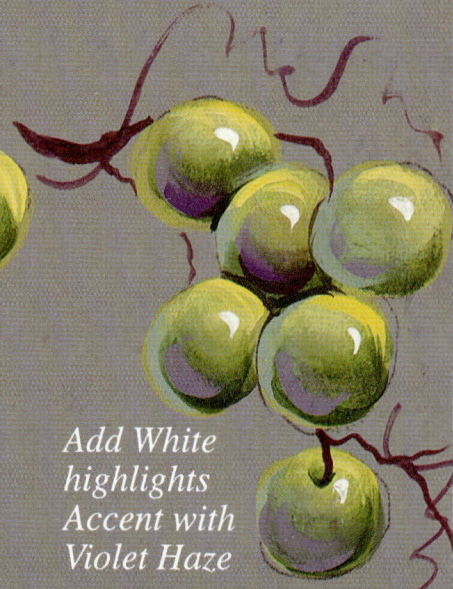

Add White
highlights
Accent with
Violet Haze

Blackberries

Paynes Grey

Napa Red

Diox. Purple

Country Blue

Tap berries using
Q-tip with Glazing Medium,
Paynes Grey,
Dioxazine Purple &
Napa Red

Shade with
Country Blue

Highlight on
right
side with
Napa Red & White
Add shine & stems

Varnish coasters with JW Satin Varnish and top with Finishing Wax. Always follow the directions on the label.

Bamboo & Dragonfly
Top of Coaster

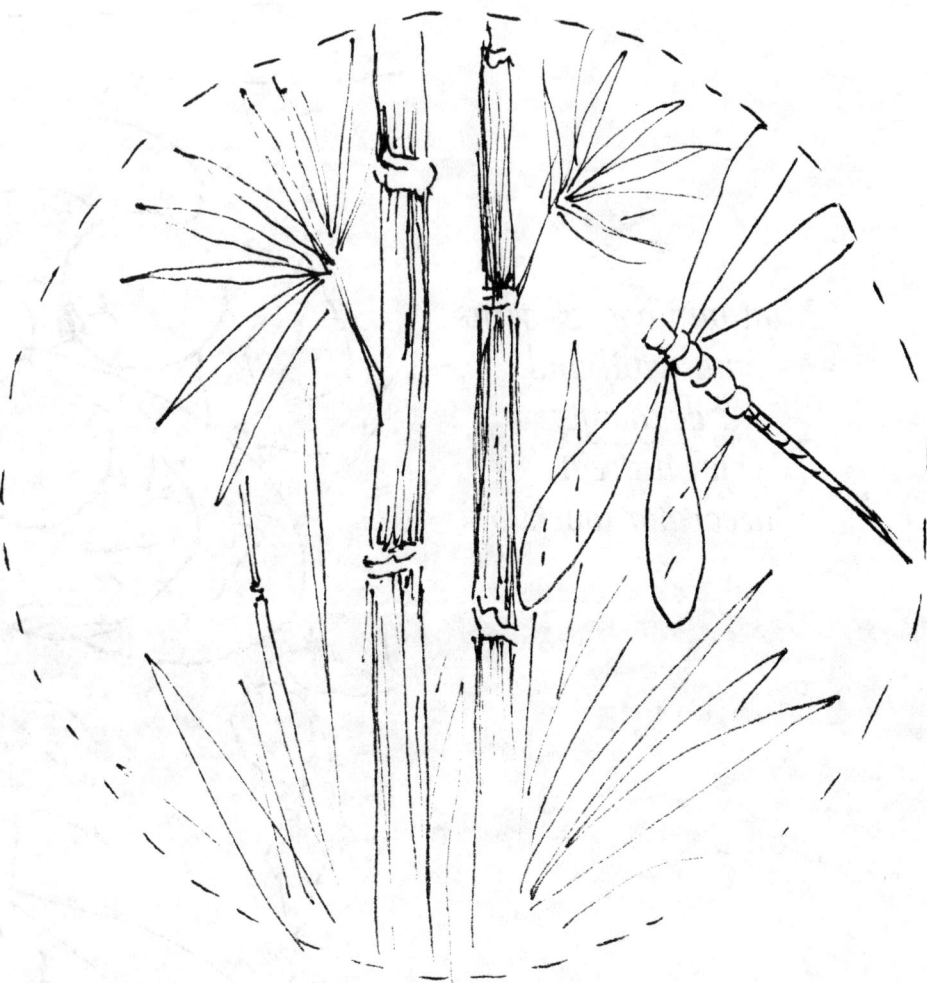

Bamboo & Dragonfly
Oval Box

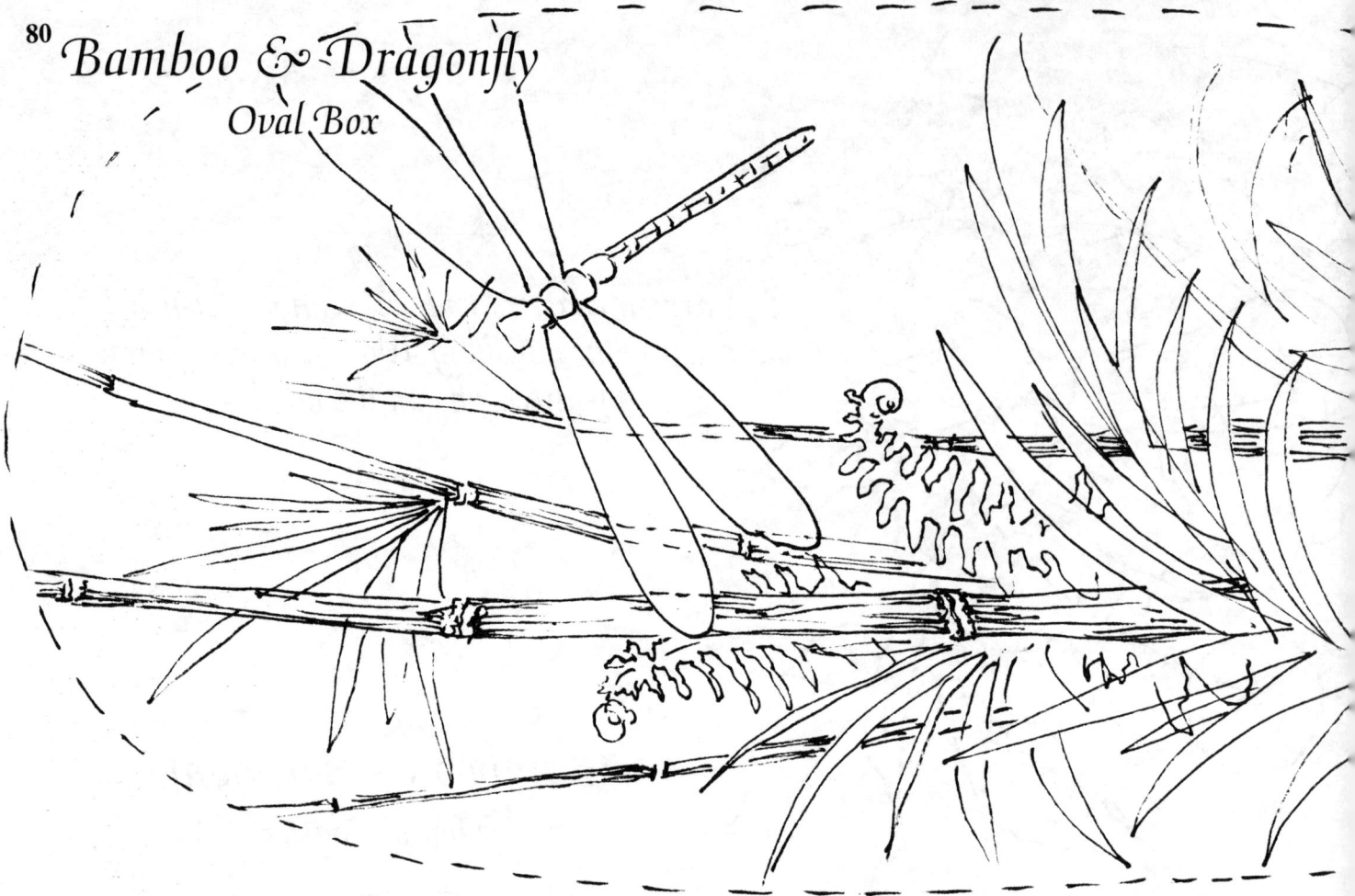

Paint bamboo & ferns
on a wall; add
a dragonfly
for a great
decorator touch.

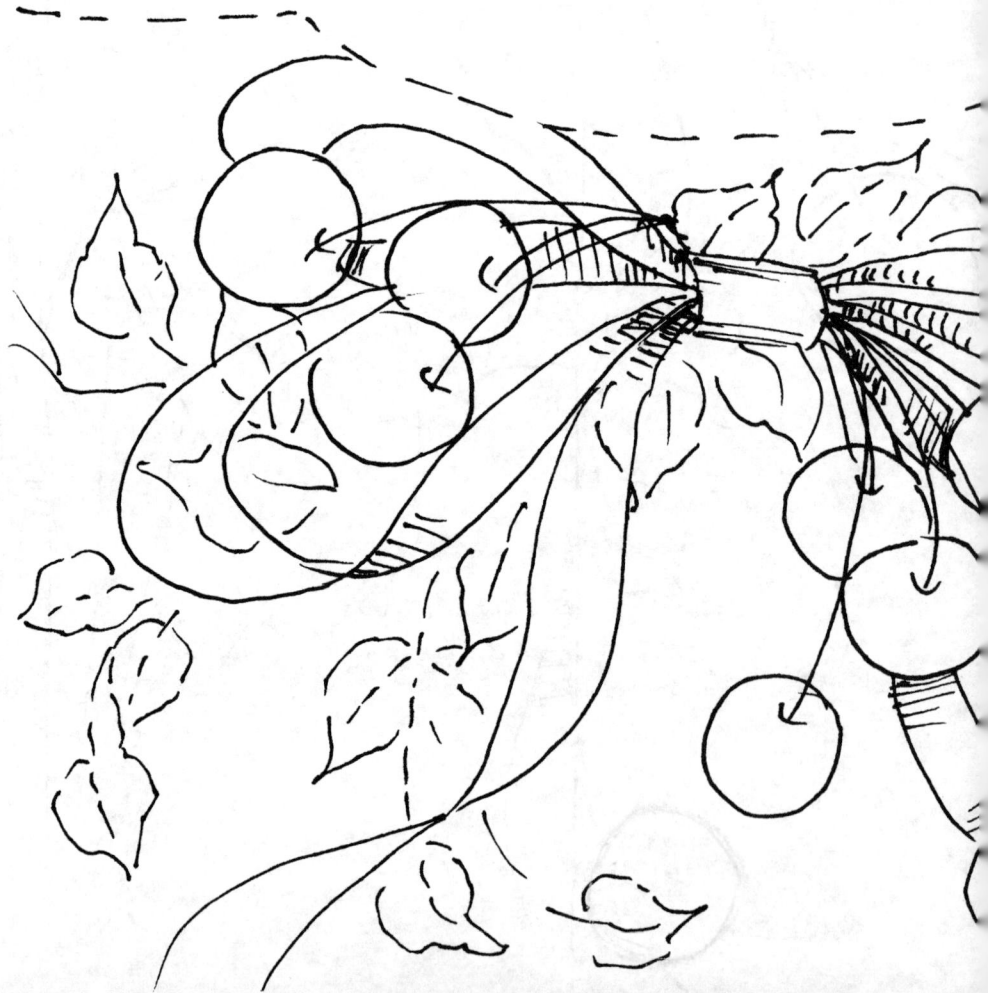

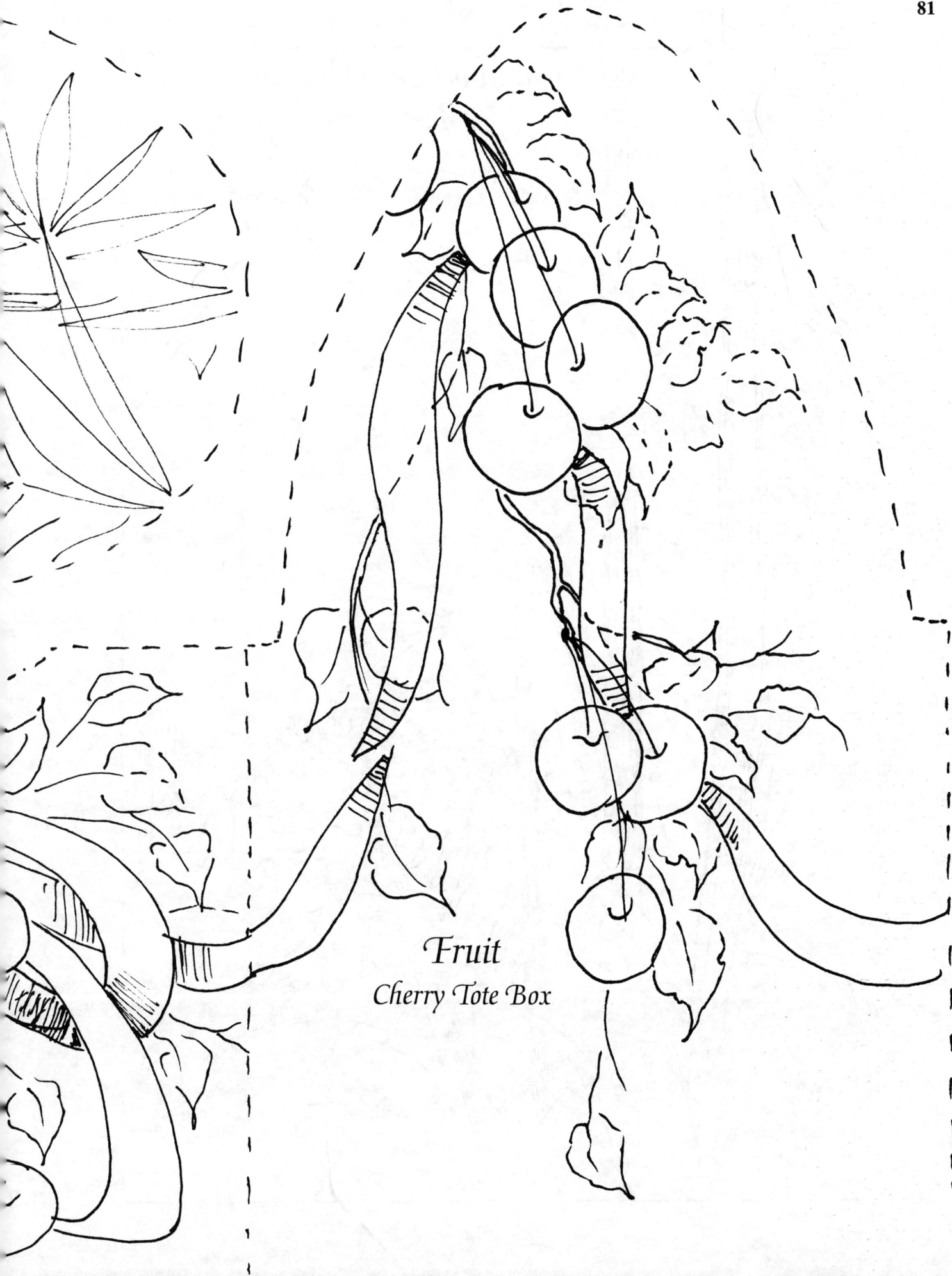

Fruit
Cherry Tote Box

82

Bamboo & Dragonfly
Mantel Clock

Bamboo and Dragonfly

Surfaces: *Mantel Clock (Stan Brown's Arts & Crafts), Oval Box (Valhala),*
Coaster Set (Cabin Crafters 1-800-669-3920)

Palette: DecoArt Americana Acrylic

DA001 Titanium White	*DA052 Avocado*	*DA056 Olive Green*
DA064 Burnt Umber	*DA082 Evergreen*	*DA093 Raw Sienna*
DA101 Dioxazine Purple	*DA152 Shale Green*	*DA178 Blue Mist*
DA167 Paynes Grey	*Faux Glazing Medium*	

Preparation: Paint the box with Scheewe Gesso. Clock face and coaster box, **J W White Lightning**.

Bamboo: Create bamboo stalks with edge of 1/2" angle shader varing the colors using **Glazing Medium, Avocado, Evergreen, Raw Sienna** and touches of **Dioxazine Purple**.

Ferns: Tap ferns with **Avocado, Evergreen, Olive Green,** and **Blue Mist** using a 2/0 or 10/0 fan brush. Vary the colors adding lots of **Glazing Medium** to create some transparent effects.

Grass: Pull large grasses with the edge of an angle shader. Paint fine grasses with a liner.

Dragonfly: Trace and transfer dragon fly with white or gray graphite. Paint body with **Olive Green**, Shade with **Avocado** and highlight with **Olive Green** with a little **Titanium White**. Detail wings with **Paynes Grey** using a liner brush. Paint transparent glaze of color over wings with **Glazing Medium** and a tiny bit **Dioxazine Purple**.

Leaves Leaves

Surfaces: *Sewing Box (Stan Brown's Arts and Crafts), Switch Plate (Hardware store), Trash Bin (Russ Hayden), Old Book, Wooden Plate & Candles*

Paints: DecoArt Americana

DA001 Titanium White	*DA052 Avocado*	*DA056 Olive Green*
DA064 Burnt Umber	*DA082 Evergreen*	*DA148 Emperor's Gold*
DA158 Antique Teal	*DA178 Blue Mist*	*Faux Glazing Medium*

Basecoats: **JW White Lightning**

Pattern: Trace and transfer large leaves and branches as needed.

Branches: **Burnt Umber** and **Faux Glazing Medium**.

Squishy Leaves: **Faux Glazing Medium, Evergreen, Avocado, Blue Mist** and **Emperor's Gold**.

Basic Leaves: **Avocado, Evergreen, Olive Green** and **Blue Mist**.

Ribbon: **Blue Mist, Antique Teal, Titanium White** and **Faux Glazing Medium**.

Stems and Squiggles: **Blue Mist** and **Olive Green**.

Spatter: **Emperor's Gold**.

Leaves Leaves
Switch Plate

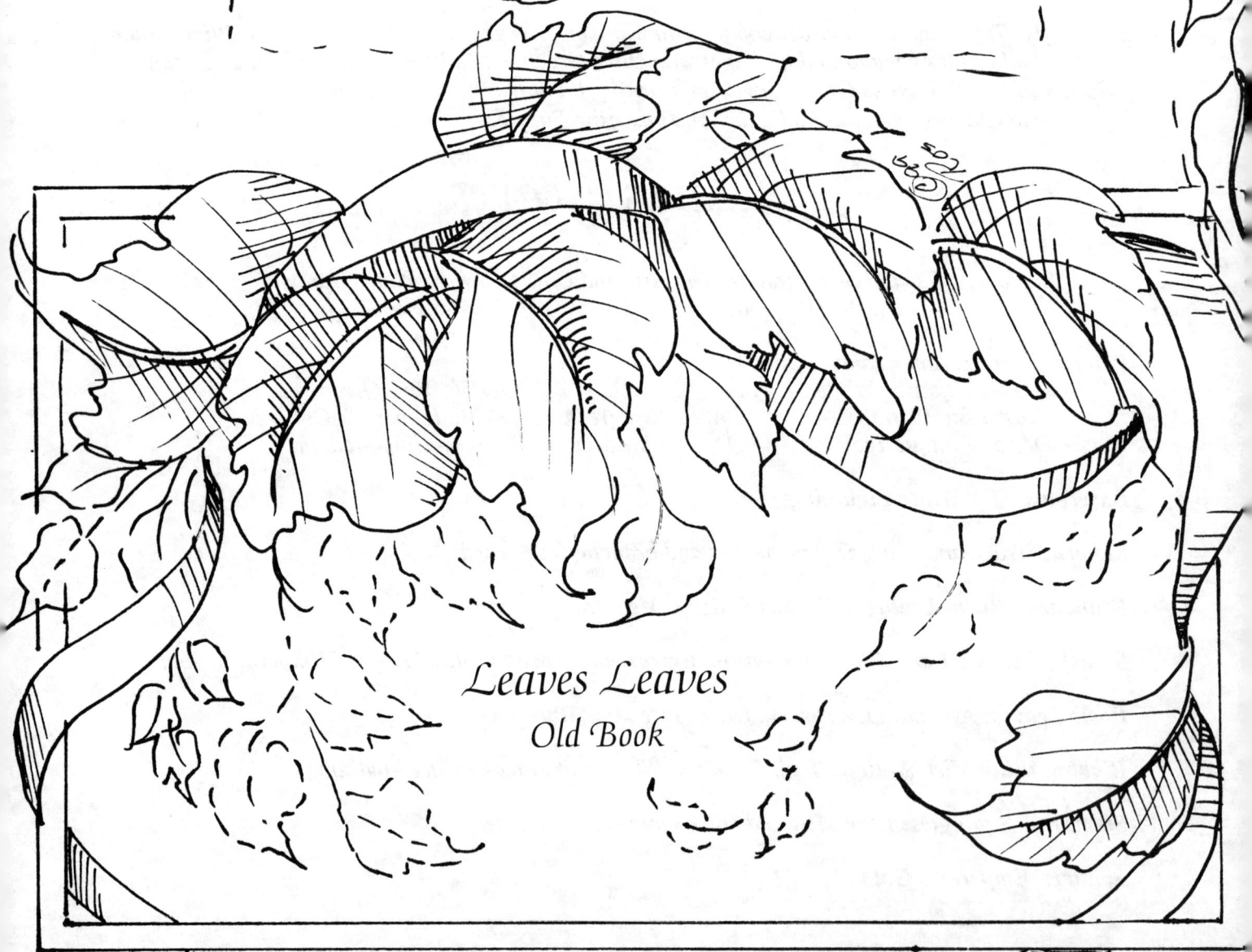

Leaves Leaves
Old Book

BAMBOO & DRAGONFLY
COASTERS
OVAL BOX
MANTEL CLOCK
PAGES 79 - 83

LEAVES LEAVES
SEWING BOX
SWITCH PLATE
TRASH BIN
OLD BOOK
WOODEN PLATE & CANDLES
PAGES 83 - 89

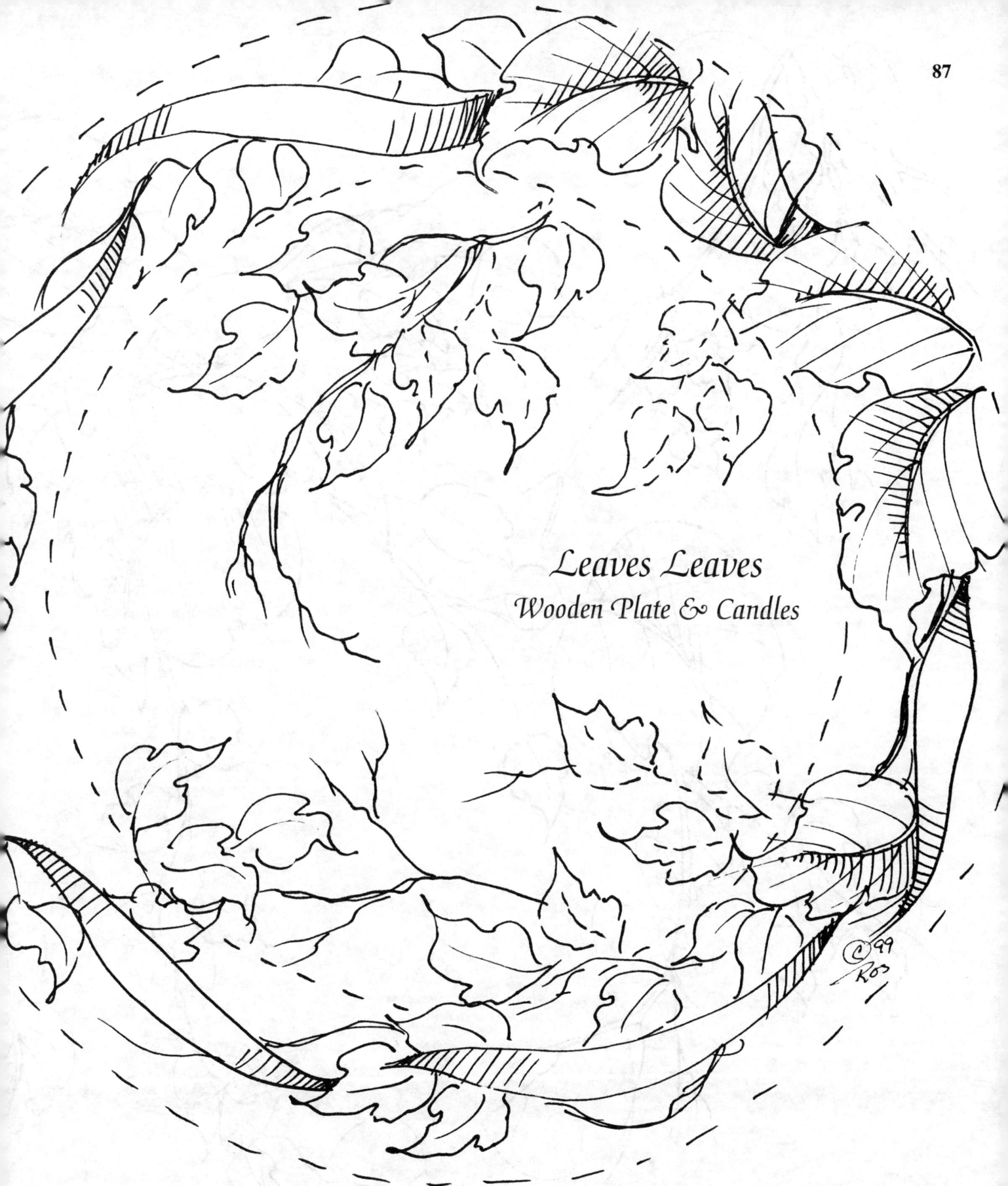

Leaves Leaves
Wooden Plate & Candles

88

Leaves Leaves
Wooden Trash Bin

Leaves Leaves

Sewing Box
Front of Sewing Box, repeat
on back lid.

Gran's Cottage

Surfaces: *Table (Wayneswood), Scalloped Door Crown (Stephís Folk Art Studio)*

Paints: DecoArt Americana

DA001 Titanium White	DA011 Lemon Yellow	DA024 Hi Lite Flesh
DA052 Avocado	DA056 Olive Green	DA063 Burnt Sienna
DA064 Burnt Umber	DA082 Evergreen	DA101 Dioxazine Purple
DA141 Blue Violet	DA149 Silver Sage Green	DA151 Royal Fuchsia
DA167 Paynes Grey	DA178 Blue Mist	DA190 Winter Blue
DA193 Blue Chiffon	Faux Glazing Medium	

Basecoats: *Paint door crown and table with one coat of* **White Lightning**. *Sand lightly.*

Sky: *Tape inside edge of signboard with masking tape to keep edges clean. Paint lower sky with* **Hi-Lite Flesh** *blending into* **Blue Chiffon** *and* **Winter Blue**.

Gran's Cottage
Table Top
Adjust pattern to fit scalloped door crown.

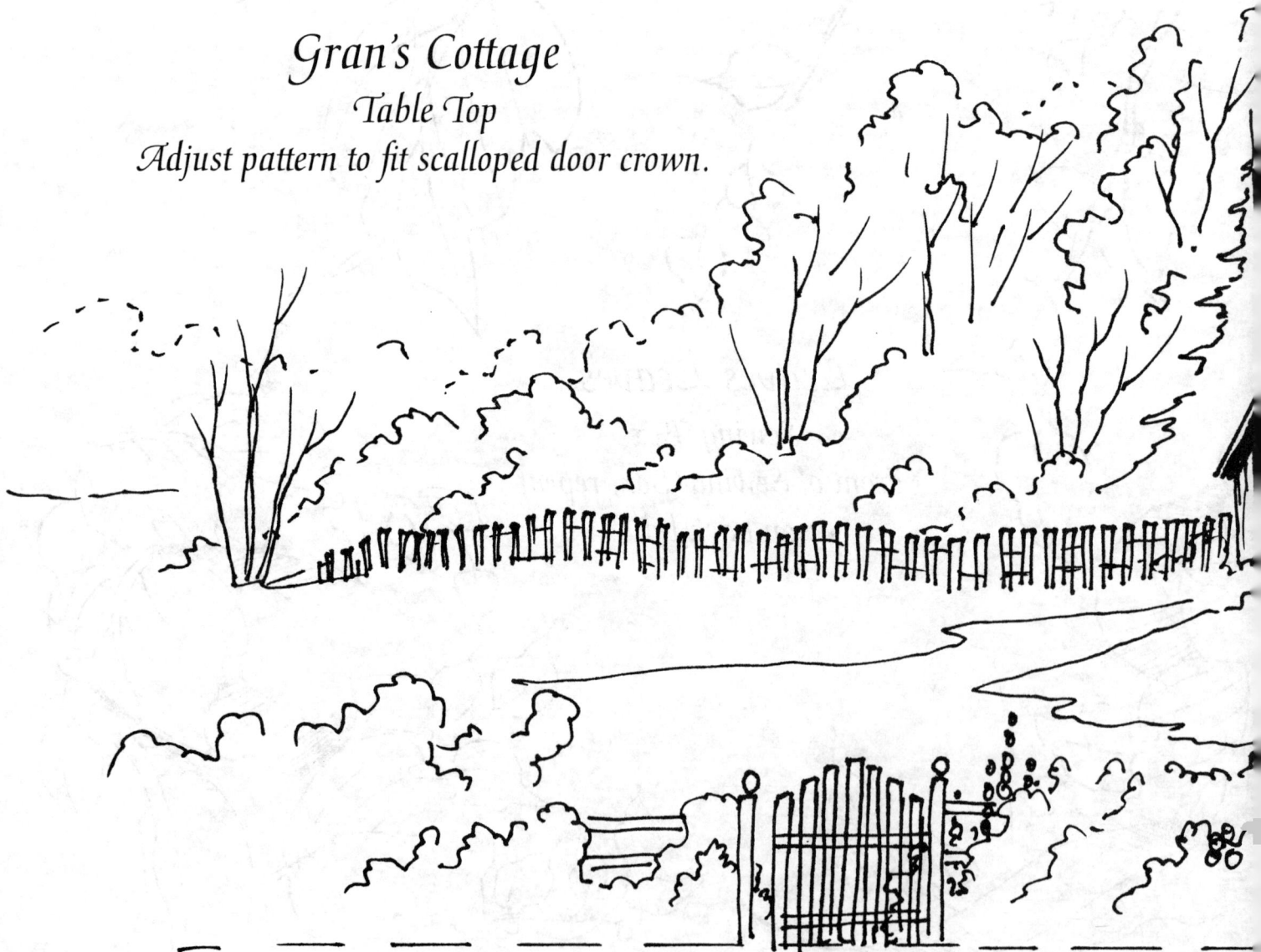

Distant Foliage: *Tap foliage with **Glazing Medium**, **Hi-Lite Flesh**, **Violet Haze**, and **Winter Blue**. Vary the colors and keep pale and distant. Add a little **Blue Mist** and **Avocado** to sky color to create a second layer of foliage.*

Pattern: *Trace and transfer the birdhouses and lettering with gray graphite.*

Cottage: *Base cottage with a brush mix of **Burnt Umber** and **Winter Blue**. Paint around windows and door. Leave tiny space at roof edges so that you know where parts are.*

*Paint right wall and cast shadow under the eves with **Burnt Umber**. Drag **Winter Blue** over the **Burnt Umber** leaving the space for the cast shadow. Drag **Hi-Lite Flesh** over the sunny left walls leaving the cast shadow. Pull a little **Winter Blue** mixed with **Glazing Medium** in the cast shadows. Paint board lines with **Burnt Umber** and **Paynes Grey** with your liner brush starting at the edge of the roof.*

Gran's Cottage continued

*Paint roof with little pull down strokes with **Burnt Umber**, **Burnt Sienna**, **Winter Blue** and **Hi-Lite Flesh** using a #4 or #6 Flat shader. Hop around pulling strokes like the slant of the roof to create shingles.*

*Paint under eaves and in the windows with a mix of **Paynes Grey** and **Burnt Umber** using a liner brush. Detail windows with the color of that wall and add edgeboards. Glaze a little **Paynes Grey** and **Glazing Medium** on the right roof. Add touches of **Burnt Sienna** and **Glazing Medium** on the light walls. Paint a little **Winter Blue** and **Glazing Medium** in the right sides of the windows.*

Gran's Cottage
Left side of Table Top

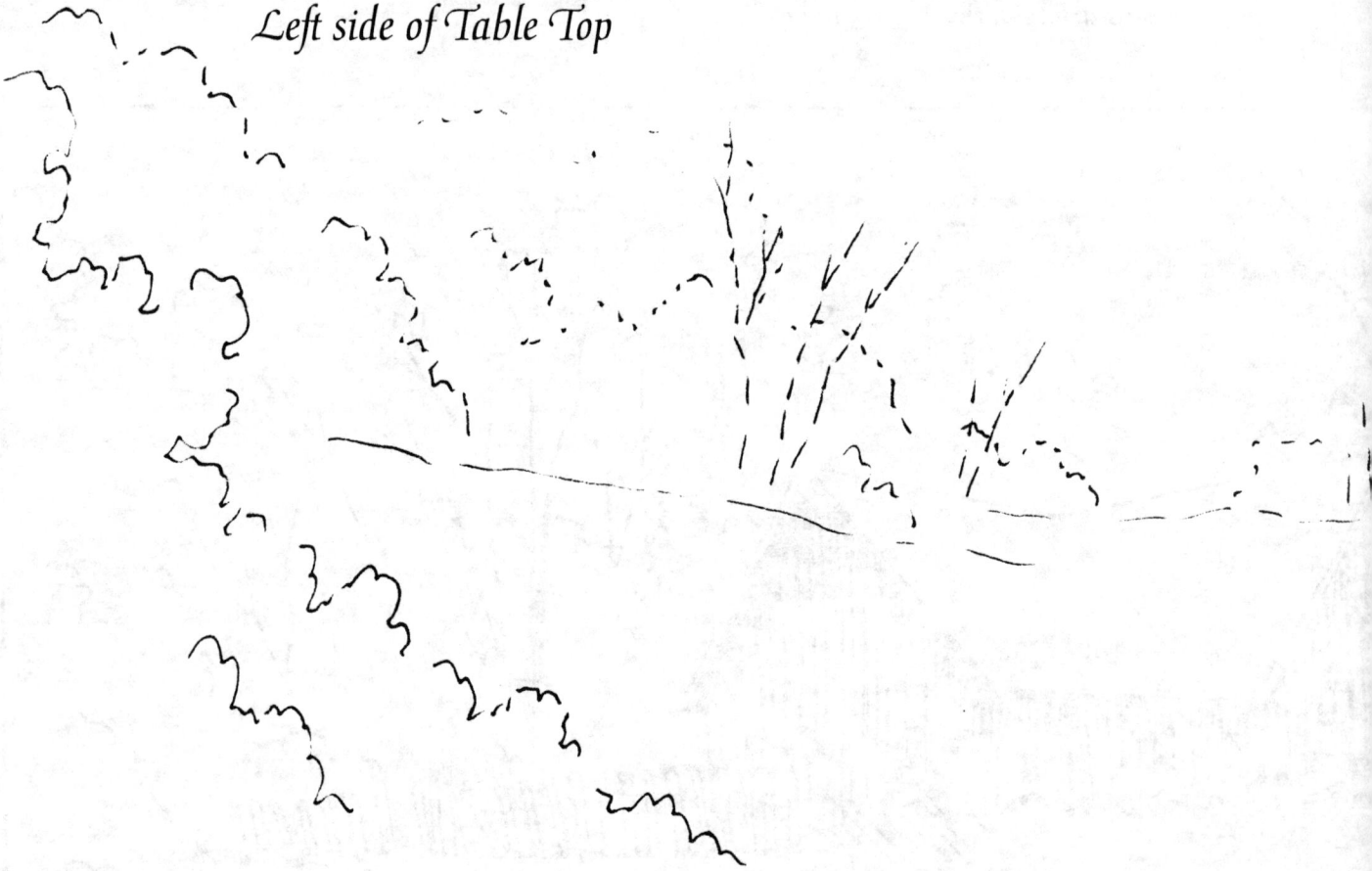

Gran's Cottage
Leaves on Table

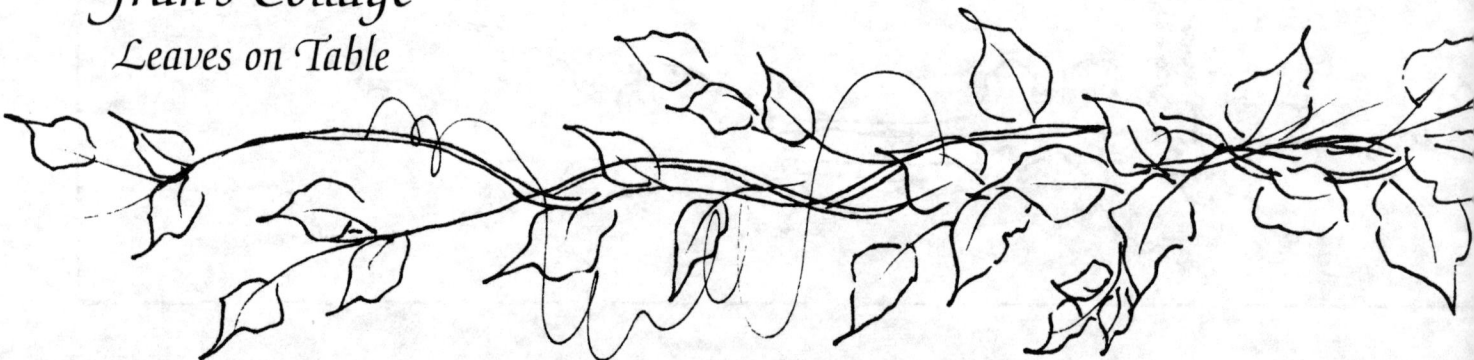

Gran's Cottage continued

Land and Grass: *Paint land areas starting at the top with **Hi-Lite Flesh**, **Blue Chiffon**, **Olive Green** and **Blue Mist**, brushing across with the chisel edge of your flat or angle shaded. Vary the colors starting with the lightest value and gradually getting darker. Paint the grass area in front of the cottage with the same colors using tiny pull down strokes with a 2/0 fan brush. Paint shadow at the right end of cottage with **Blue Mist**.*
*Paint path with streaky color with **Hi-Lite Flesh** and **Burnt Umber**.*

Foreground Foliage: *Tap foliage with **Avocado**, **Evergreen**, **Colonial Green** and **Olive Green**.*

Bushes: *Tap tiny bush in front of Cottage with **Avocado**. Highlight on the left side with **Olive Green** and **Blue Mist** on the right side of the house. Tap flowers with the tip of your liner.*

Flowers: *Paint spiky flowers with **Blue Violet**, **Dioxazine Purple** and **Titanium White** using a liner brush. Tap some areas with **Blue Violet** and **Titanium White** using 1/2" foliage Brush. Tap a few touches of **Lemon Yellow**.*

Window Box Flowers: *Tap a little **Avocado** with the tip of your liner. Paint dot flowers with **Royal Fuchsia** and **Titanium White**.*

Gate: *Paint gate and fence with **Hi-Lite Flesh** using your liner brush.*

Finishing Touches: *Paint fine grass lines with **Olive Green**. Spatter with **Titanium White** mixed with water.*

Paint spray of "squishy leaves across the front of the drawer.

Adjust gardens around the cottage to make this design fit any surface. Great "Welcome" sign to put at your front door.

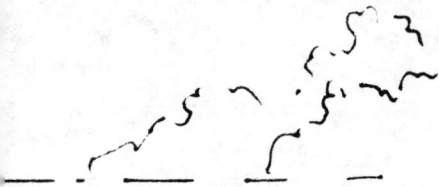

Christmas Floorcloth
Left Side

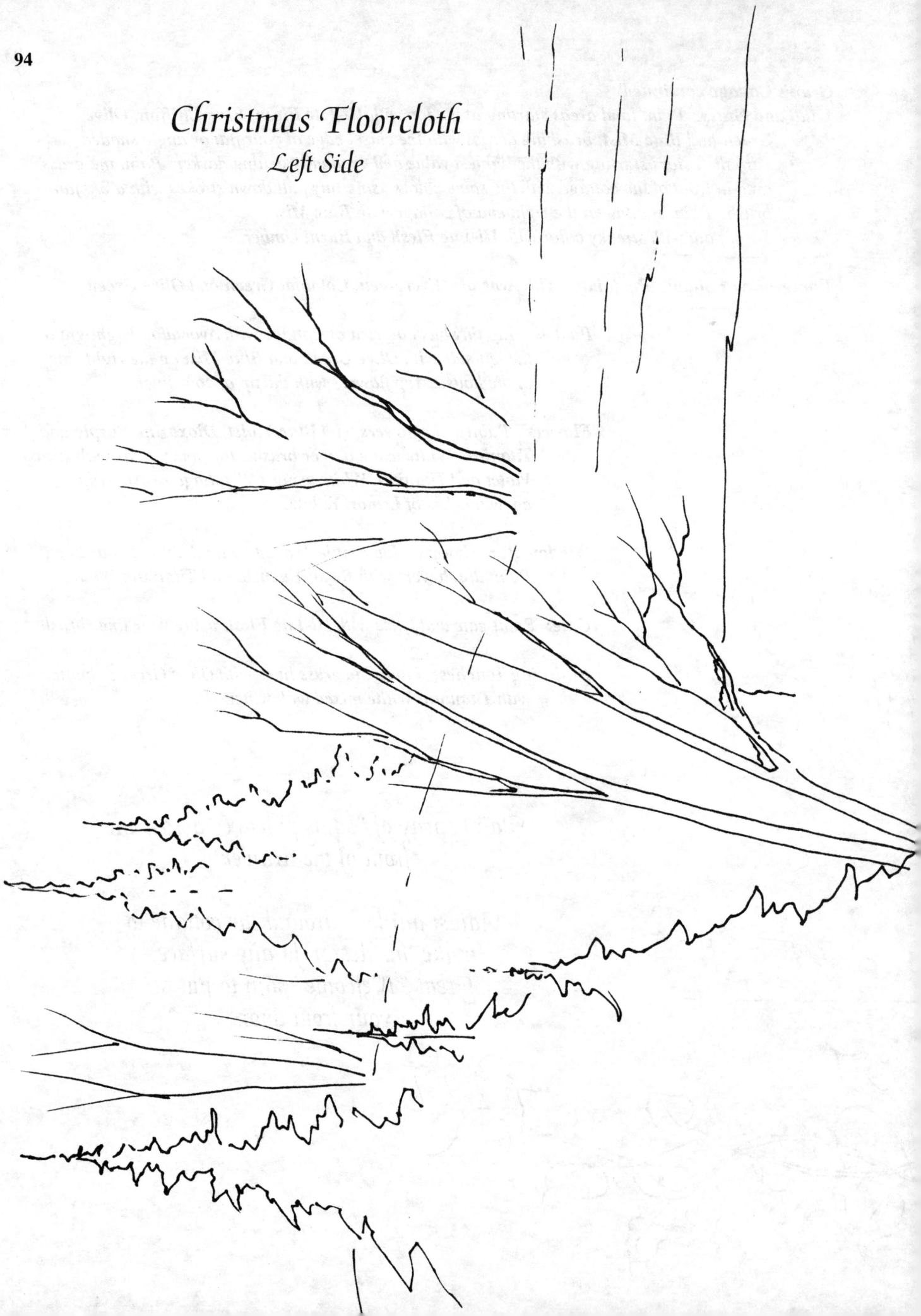

Baskets

Burnt Umber

Camel

Raw
Sienna

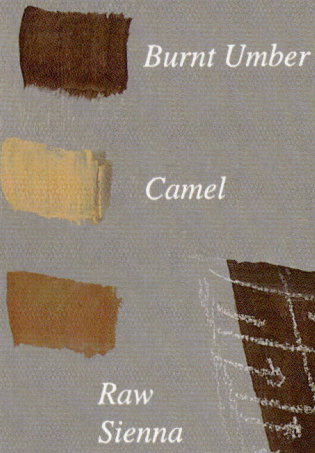

Base Basket & handle
with Burnt Umber

Paint vertical lines
with Raw Sienna
Paint weave with Camel &
Raw Sienna
Shade weave with
Burnt Umber &
Glazing Medium

Blue Mist

Bows

Titanium White

Antique White

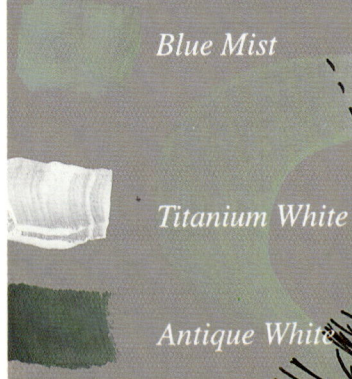

Pull ribbon strokes with
Glazing Medium & Blue Mist
Shade with Antique Teal
Highlight with Titanium White

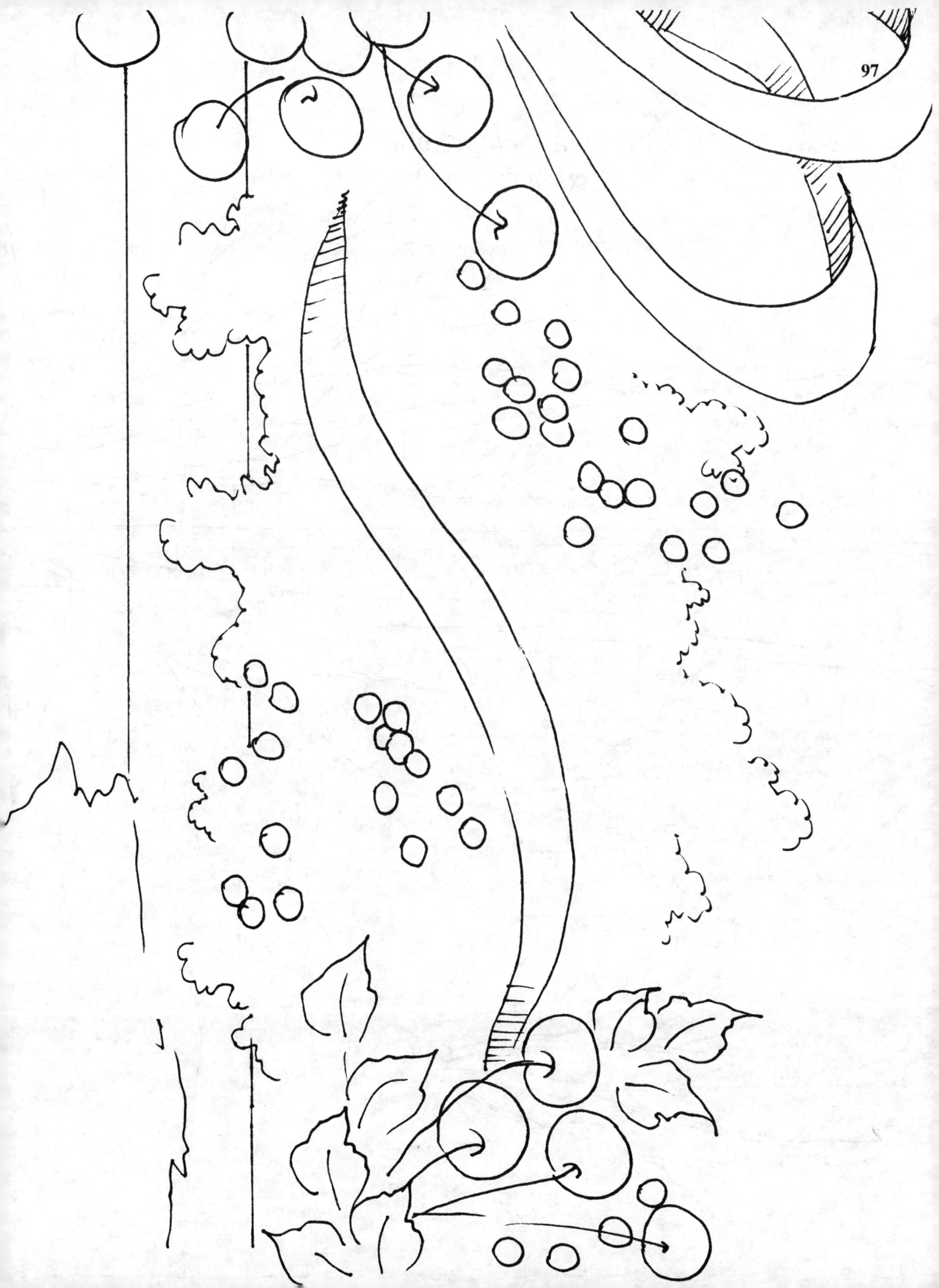

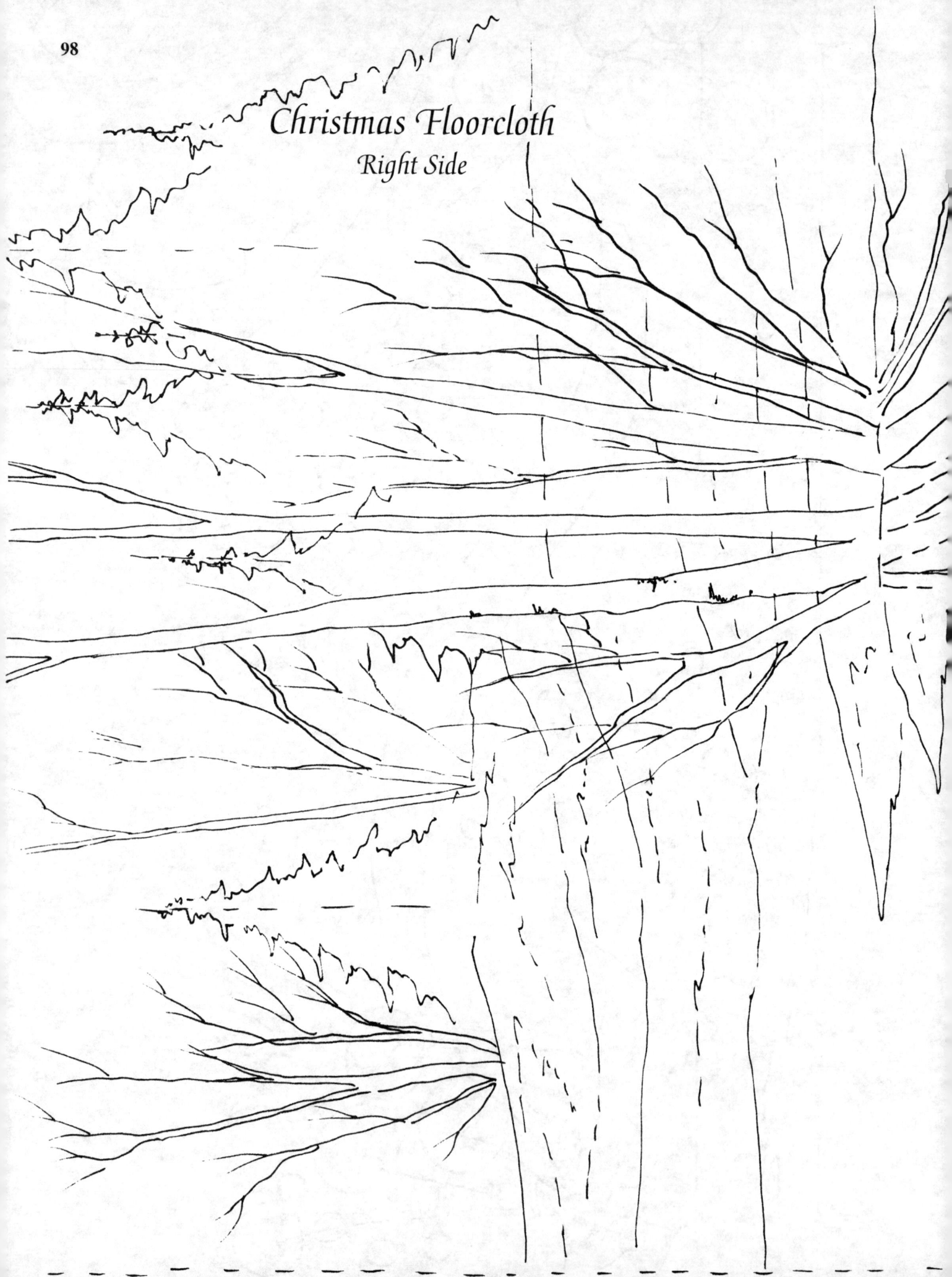

Christmas Floorcloth
Right Side

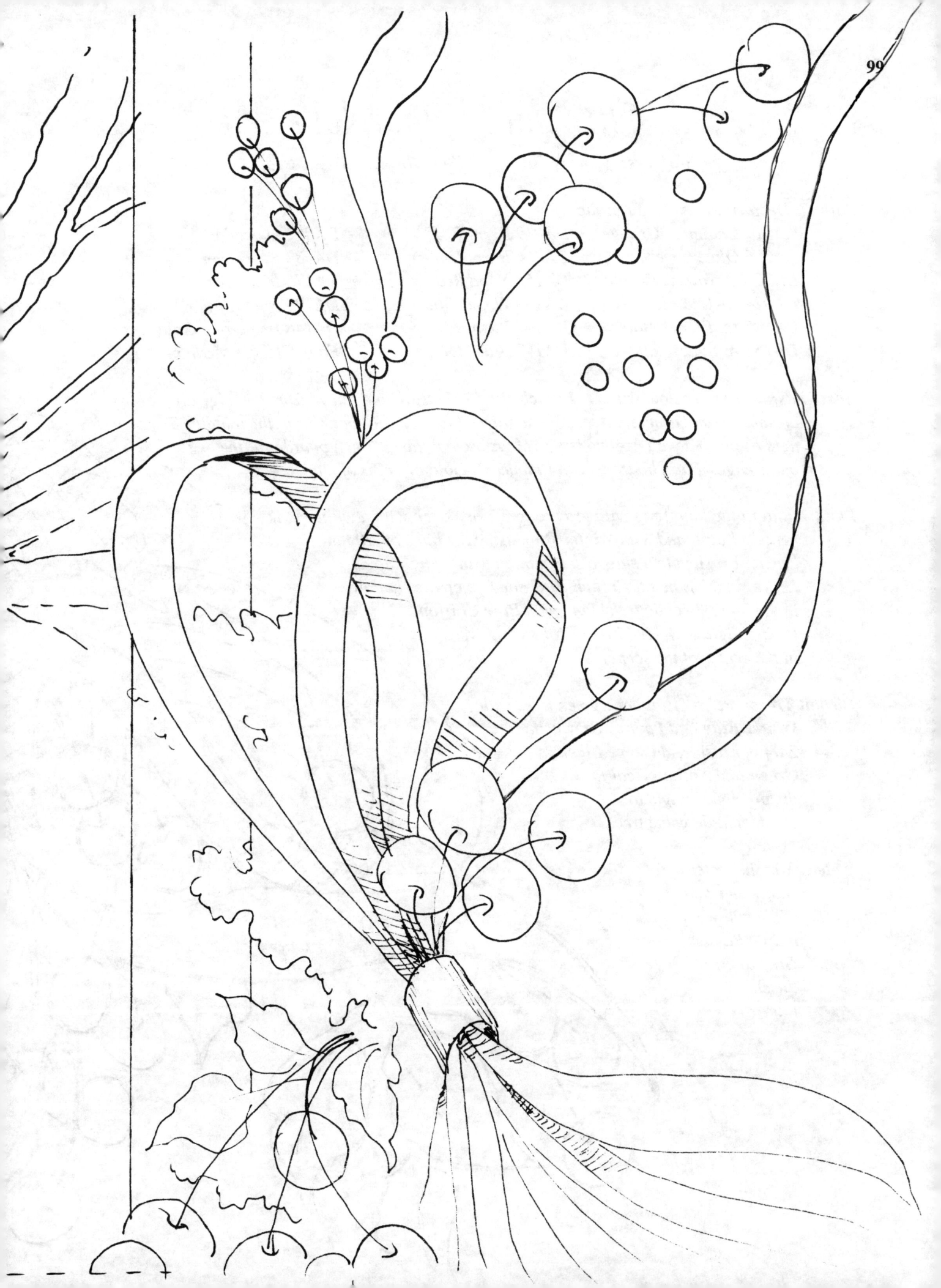

Christmas Floorcloth

Surfaces: Canvas Floorcloth (Stan Brown's Arts & Crafts)

Paints: DecoArt Americana Acrylic

DA014 Cadmium Orange	DA019 Berry Red	DA052 Avocado
DA056 Olive Green	DA064 Burnt Umber	DA082 Evergreen
DA101 Dioxazine Purple	DA165 Napa Red	DA178 Blue Mist
DA024 Hi-Lite Flesh	DA190 Winter Blue	DA193 Blue Chiffon
DA185 Lt. French Blue	DA167 Paynes Grey	DA148 Emperor's Gold
DA158 Antique Teal	DA157 Black Green	Faux Glazing Medium

Basecoats: Base floorcloth with **Lt. French Blue**. Measure and tap 7" from the edge all the way around. Trim corners. Measure and tape 6" to create 1" boarder in the middle. Trim corners as needed with a xacto knife. Measure and tape 2" inch boarder at the outer edge. Paint boarder with **Emperor's Gold** or color of choice.

Land: Pattern the land lines with gray graphite or sketch with a white chalk pencil. Paint land with **Winter Blue** using the back of 2/0 fan brush. Brush with a side to side motion using a light touch. Leave some of the **Lt. French Blue** show to create shadows in the land. Highlight the land with **Blue Chiffon**. Re-highlight with **Hi-Lite Flesh** in a few areas in the center of the scene.

Distant Trees: Paint distant evergreen trees with **Winter Blue** and **Paynes Grey** using 2/0 fan brush. Add some **Black Green** and **Antique Teal** to the previous mingle to create middle value trees.

Water: Wet the water area with water and while still wet put a little **Paynes Grey** along the shore line.

Poinsettia Door Crown

Left Side

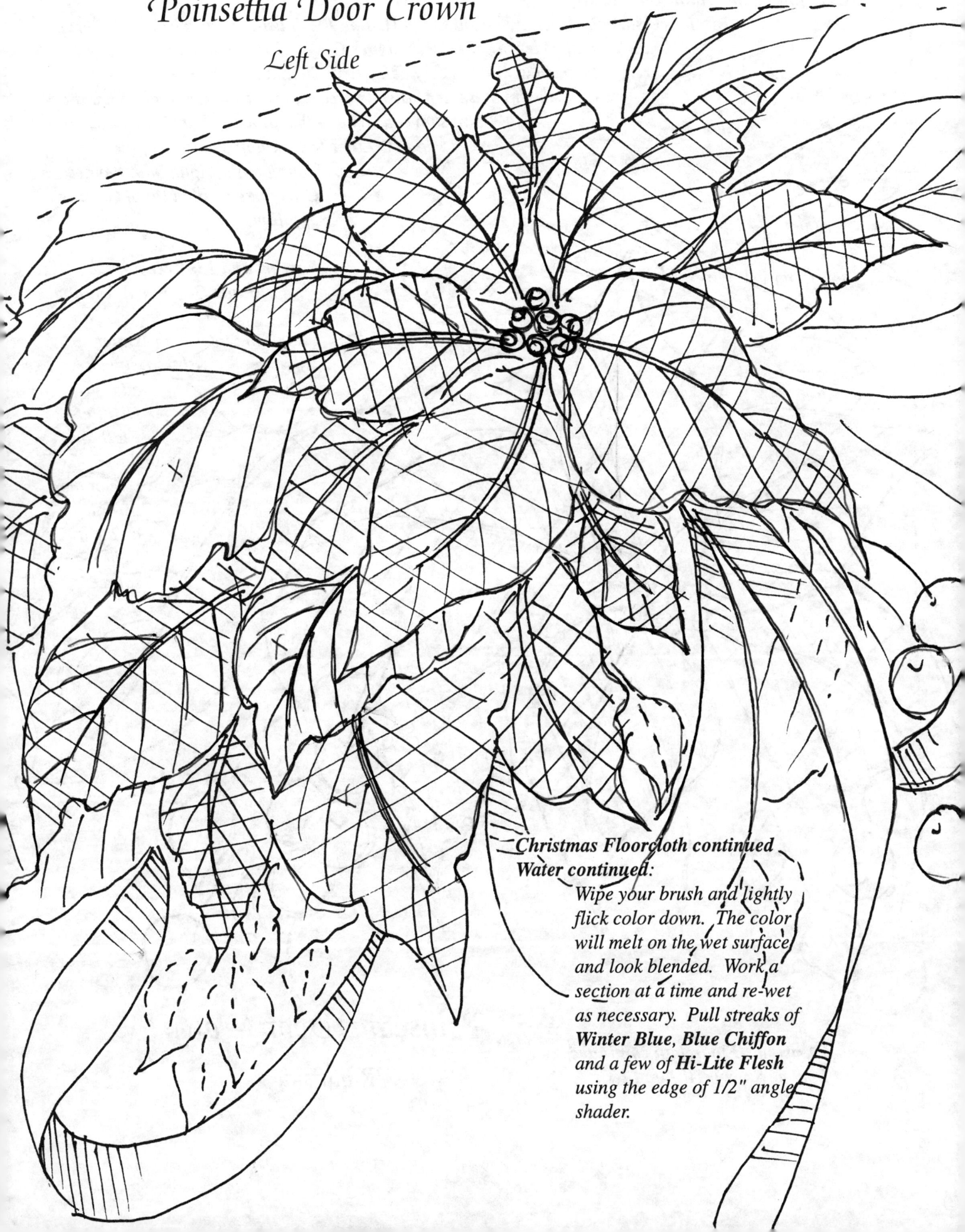

Christmas Floorcloth continued
Water continued:

Wipe your brush and lightly
flick color down. The color
will melt on the wet surface
and look blended. Work a
section at a time and re-wet
as necessary. Pull streaks of
Winter Blue, Blue Chiffon
and a few of **Hi-Lite Flesh**
using the edge of 1/2" angle
shader.

102

Christmas Floorcloth continued

Birch Trees: Paint birch tree trunks with **Hi-Lite Flesh** using a liner brush. Paint branches with **Burnt Umber** and **Paynes Grey**. Wet a section of tree trunk and touch with **Burnt Umber**, **Burnt Sienna** and **Paynes Grey** using the tip of a liner brush to create the marking on the birch bark. Paint snow on some of the branches with **Winter Blue** and **Hi-Lite Flesh**. Paint shadows of these trees, slanting to the right, with **Paynes Gray** mixed with a lot of **Glazing Medium**.

Foreground Fir Trees: **Black Green** and **Antique Teal**. Paint snow on all the trees with **Winter Blue** first then add **Hi-Lite Flesh** on the left side of the snow to create a light source.

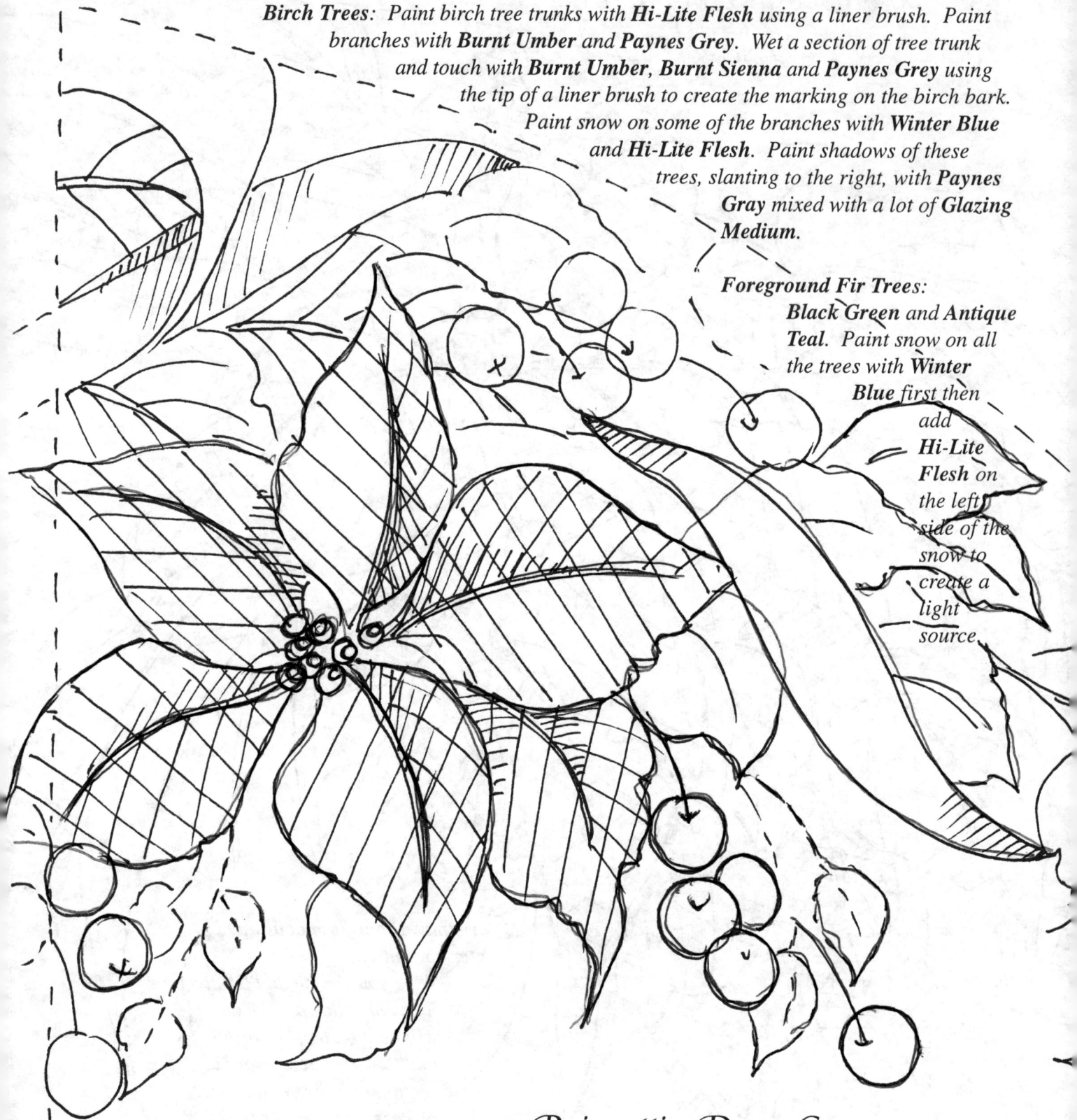

Christmas Floorcloth continued
Spatter Snow: Hi-Lite Flesh.

Poinsettia Door Crown
Right side

Poinsettia Door Crown

Surface: Door Crown (Russ Hayden)

Palette: DecoArt Americana Acrylic
DA001 Titanium White   DA010 Cadmium Yellow   DA052 Avocado
DA056 Olive Green   DA082 Evergreen   DA178 Blue Mist
DA014 Cadmium Orange   DA019 Berry Red   DA165 Napa Red
DA101 Dioxazine Purple   DA148 Emperor's Gold
Faux Glazing Medium

Basecoats: Paint signboard with one coat of **White Lightning**. Sand lightly.

Pattern: Trace and transfer pattern for poinsettias and large leaves using gray graphite. Transfer berries and ribbons as needed. It is best to freehand pale squishy leaves, as it is difficult to cover graphite lines with transparent leaves.

Squishy Leave: Paint squishy leaves with **Avocado, Evergreen, Olive Green, Blue Mist,** and **Glazing Medium**. Paint largest leaves with # 18 or 20 (3/4") flat brush. Paint smaller leaves with a #12 flat shader.

Leaves: **Avocado, Evergreen, Olive Green** and **Blue Mist**.

Poinsettias: Poinsettias are red leaves. Base with **Berry Red**. Highlight with **Cadmium Orange** and **Titanium White**. Shade with **Napa Red** and **Dioxazine Purple**. Paint veins with **Napa Red**. Paint dots of **Cadmium Yellow** with the end of a paintbrush and add dot of **Berry Red** on top of each for the center of the flowers.

Ribbon: Berry Red, Cadmium Orange, Titanium White, Napa Red, Dioxazine Purple and Glazing Medium.

Berries: Base berries with **Olive Green**. Shade with **Blue Mist** and **Evergreen**. Highlight with **Cadmium Yellow** and **Titanium White**.

Finishing Touches: Paint stems and squiggles with **Avocado**. Spatter and edge board with **Emperor's Gold**. Tint edges and around design with **Blue Mist** and **Glazing Medium**.

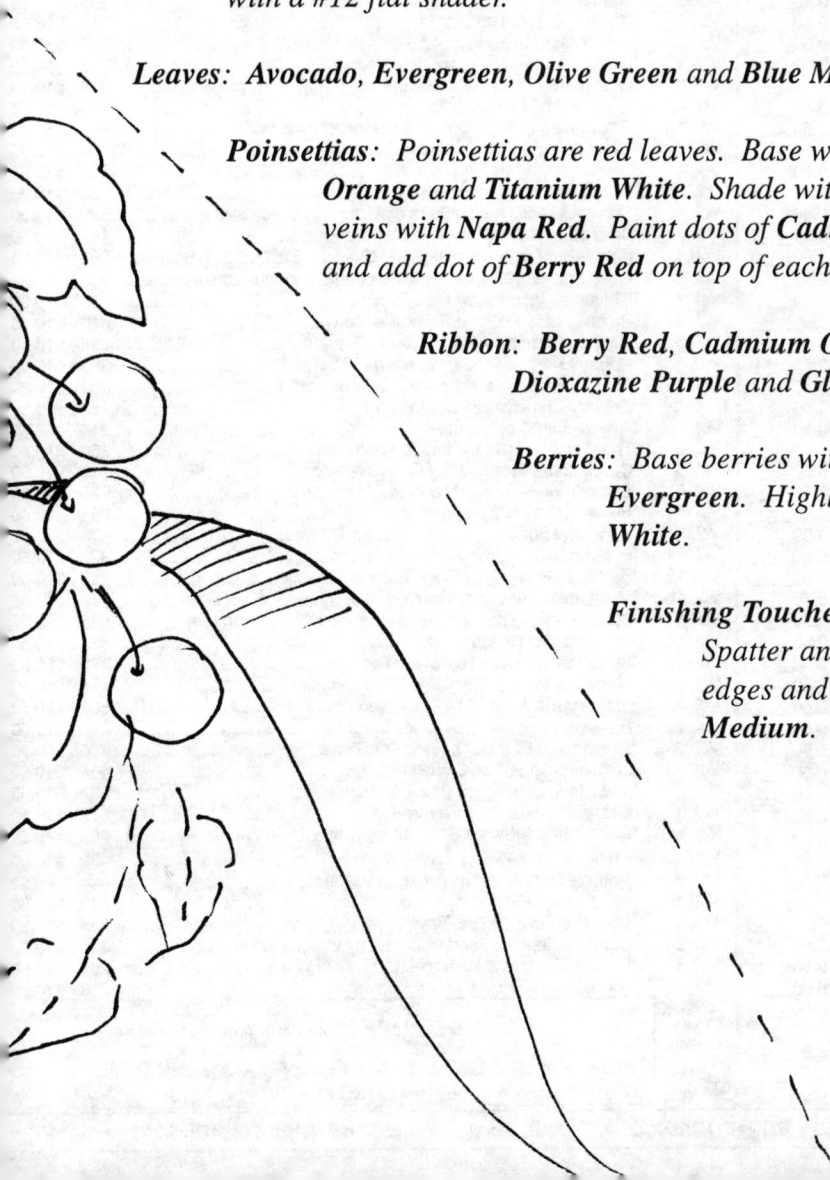

Susan Scheewe Publications Inc. 4-30-03

13435 N.E. Whitaker Way Portland, Or. 97230 PH (503)254-9100 FAX (503)252-9508 Orders Only (800)796-1953

ACRYLIC BOOKS

	Title	#	Price
Vol. 1	"The Garden Path" by Sandi Brady Archer	492	$10.50
Vol. 1	"How Delicious" by Elaina Appleby......*NEW*	541	$10.50
Vol. 2	'Country Heartworks 2" by Reed Baxter	365	$10.50
Vol. 2	"The Flower Market" by Joyce Benner	319	$10.50
Vol. 3	"Acrylic Painting The Easy Way" by Bill Blackman	460	$10.50
Vol. 1	"Tole-tilly Tickled" by Lisa Brownie & Gina Knighton	490	$10.50
Vol. 3	"Country Fixin's - For All Seasons" by Rhonda Caldwell	332	$10.50
Vol. 1	"Country Celebration" by Tammy Christensen	378	$10.50
Vol. 1	"Folkart Friends" by Darcy Christensen	437	$10.50
Vol. 1	"Holly Berries and Twigs" by Kim Christmas....*NEW*	549	$10.50
Vol. 1	"Season's Change" by Susan Dircks DeWenter....*NEW*	551	$10.50
Vol. 1	"A Painters Garden " by Jane Dillon	354	$10.50
Vol. 3	"A Painters Garden 3" by Jane Dillon	458	$10.50
Vol. 4	"A Painters Garden 4" by Jane Dillon....*NEW*	536	$10.50
Vol. 1	"Santas and Sams" by Bobi Dolara	258	$10.50
Vol. 2	"Vintage Peace" by Bobi Dolara	270	$10.50
Vol. 2	"Floral Designs 2" by Carol Empet	338	$10.50
Vol. 3	"Floral Portraits" by Carol Empet	358	$10.50
Vol. 1	"Angels Are Near" by Carol Freeman & Brenda Turley	375	$10.50
Vol. 2	"Briar Patch #2" by Sandy Fochler	424	$10.50
Vol. 3	"Briar Patch #3" by Sandy Fochler	456	$10.50
Vol. 4	"Briar Patch #4" by Sandy Fochler	479	$10.50
Vol. 5	"Briar Patch #5" by Sandy Fochler	506	$10.50
Vol. 1	"Between Friends-Briar Patch" by Sandy Fochler, Lorrie Dirksen, Holly Jespersen, Bonnie Morello	448	$10.50
Vol. 2	"Between Friends 2-Briar Patch"by Sandy Fochler, Lorrie Dirksen, Holly Jespersen, Bonnie Morello	473	$10.50
Vol. 2	"Deck The Halls Bauernmalerei" by Sherry Gall	391	$10.50
Vol. 1	"Pick of The Bunch" by Lola Gill....*NEW*	527	$10.50
Vol. 1	"A Bear Necessity" by Denise Girling....*NEW*	550	$10.50
Vol. 1	"Giggles and Hugs" by Sandi Goodman....*NEW*	548	$10.50
Vol. 1	"Olde Thyme Folk Art" by Teresa Gregory	390	$10.50
Vol. 1	"Maple Sugar" by Roberta Hall	444	$10.50
Vol. 3	"Maple Sugar 3" by Roberta Hall	471	$10.50
Vol. 4	"Maple Sugar 4" by Roberta Hall	481	$10.50
Vol. 5	"Maple Sugar 5" Country Jars by Roberta Hall	491	$10.50
Vol. 7	"Maple Sugar 7" by Roberta Hall	519	$10.50
Vol. 8	"Maple Sugar 8" by Roberta Hall....*NEW*	531	$10.50
Vol. 9	"Maple Sugar 9" by Roberta Hall....*NEW*	542	$10.50
Vol. 1	"Endless Seasons" by Tiffany Hastie	498	$10.50
Vol. 2	"Endless Seasons 2" by Tiffany Hastie....*NEW*	521	$10.50
Vol. 2	"A Little For Every Holiday" by Vickie Higley	477	$10.50
Vol. 1	"Garden Collection" by Bev Hink - Birdwell....*NEW*	526	$10.50
Vol. 1	"Artistic Treasures" by June Houck & Veda Parsley....*NEW*	535	$10.50
Vol. 1	"Painted Jars" by Conny Hubbard	454	$10.50
Vol. 1	"Happy Heart, Happy Home" by Cathy Jones	241	$10.50
Vol. 1	"Asako's Berry Hill Farm" by Asako Kan	515	$12.95
Vol. 2	"Asako's Berry Hill Farm 2" by Asako Kan	524	$10.50
Vol. 1	All Things Possible" by Susan Kelley....*NEW*	512	$10.50
Vol. 2	"All Things Possible 2" by Susan Kelley....*NEW*	544	$10.50
Vol. 2	"Dandelions 2" by Carla Kern	513	$10.50
Vol. 1	"Festive Collectibles" by Deborha Kerr...."Collectors Release"	279	$10.50
Vol. 2	"Serendipity Collectibles" by Deborha Kerr...."Collectors Release"	289	$10.50
Vol. 1	"Painted Memories, A Mother's Love" by Deborha Kerr	435	$10.50
Vol. 3	"Pickets & Pastimes 3, Feathered Inns" by M. & J. King	385	$10.50
Vol. 1	"For Me & My House" by Myrna King	370	$10.50
Vol. 1	"Enjoy The Seasons" By Roni LaBree	510	$12.95
Vol. 2	"Enjoy The Seasons 2" By Roni LaBree....*NEW*	538	$10.50
Vol. 1	"Huckleberry Horse" by Hanna Long	269	$10.50
Vol. 2	"Country Favorites" by Hanna Long	489	$10.50
Vol. 3	"Country Favorites 2" by Hanna Long	514	$10.50
Vol. 2	"Love Lives Here" by Mary Lynn Lewis	185	$6.50
Vol. 3	"Love Lives Here" by Mary Lynn Lewis	195	$6.50
Vol. 1	"Everything Under The Moon" by Jackie Ludwig	421	$10.50
Vol. 1	"Second Nature" by Kathy McPherson	427	$10.50
Vol. 2	"Second Nature 2" by Kathy McPherson	463	$10.50
Vol. 6	"Special Welcomes #6 Crop Keepers" by Corinne Miller	347	$10.50
Vol. 7	"Special Welcomes 7" by Corrine Miller....*NEW*	543	$10.50
Vol. 4	"Bitterroot Backroads 4" by Glenice Moore	478	$10.50
Vol. 5	"Bitterroot Backroads 5 - Painting Birds" by Glenice Moore	487	$10.50
Vol. 6	"Bitterroot Backroads 6" by Glenice Moore	511	$10.50
Vol. 7	"Bitterroot Backroads 7" by Glenice Moore....*NEW*	540	$10.50
Vol. 1	"Fruit & Flower Fantasies" by Joyce Morrison	277	$10.50
Vol. 2	"Fruit & Flower Fantasies 2" by Joyce Morrison	382	$10.50
Vol. 1	"Those Blooming Bears" by Cindy Ohama	493	$10.50
Vol. 3	"Those Blooming Bears 3" by Cindy Ohama....*NEW*	523	$10.50
Vol. 4	"Those Blooming Bears 4" by Cindy Ohama....*NEW*	547	$10.50
Vol. 1	"Whimsical Critters" by Lori Ohlson	228	$7.50
Vol. 2	"Sunflower Farm" by Lori Ohlson	326	$10.50
Vol. 1	"Seasons Delight" by Jurate Okura	500	$10.50
Vol. 2	"Season's Delight 2" by Jurate Okura	522	$10.50
Vol. 1	"Friends Forevermore" by Karen Ortman	434	$10.50
Vol. 3	"Friends Forevermore 3 - Kitchen & More" by Karen Ortman	509	$10.50
Vol. 1	"Holiday Medley" by Nina Owens	265	$10.50
Vol. 2	"Another Holiday Medley" by Nina Owens	296	$10.50
Vol. 1	"Gifts & Graces" by Charlene Pena	475	$10.50
Vol. 2	"Gifts & Graces 2" by Charlene Pena	497	$10.50
Vol. 3	"Gifts & Graces 3" by Charlene Pena....*NEW*	534	$10.50
Vol. 3	"Tailfeathers 3" by Gisele Pope & Carla Kern	476	$10.50
Vol. 8	"Now & Then" by La Rae Parry	428	$10.50
Vol. 1	"Between The Vines" by Jamie Mills Price	400	$10.50
Vol. 2	"Between The Vines 2" by Jamie Mills Price	419	$10.50
Vol. 4	"Between The Vines 4" by Jamie Mills Price	474	$12.95
Vol. 1	"Forever In My Heart" by Diane Richards.....AC/Fabric	188	$6.50
Vol. 2	"Memories In My Heart" by Diane Richards.....AC/Fabric	189	$6.50
Vol. 3	"Forever In My Heart II" by Diane Richards.....AC/Fabric	205	$10.50
Vol. 7	"Nostalgic Dreams" by Diane Richards	273	$10.50
Vol. 8	"Heavenly Treasures" by Diane Richards	472	$10.50
Vol. 1	"Country Classics" by Karen Rideout	413	$10.50
Vol. 2	"Country Classics 2" by Karen Rideout	465	$10.50
Vol. 1	"Country Fun For Chistmas" by Tina Rodrigues	367	$10.50
Vol. 2	"Country Fun 2" by Tina Rodrigues	383	$10.50
Vol. 3	"Country At Heart" by Tina Rodrigues	401	$10.50
Vol. 4	"Country At Heart 4" by Tina Rodrigues	410	$10.50
Vol. 1	"Painting In The Spirit" by Jill Paris Rody....*NEW*	529	$10.50
Vol. 1	"Kracker Jack Kritters" by Kathie Rueger	405	$10.50
Vol. 4	"Keepsake Sampler" by Susan & Camille Scheewe	200	$10.50
Vol. 1	"Schoolhouse Treasures" by Cathy Schmidt	408	$10.50
Vol. 2	"Schoolhouse Treasures 2" by Cathy Schmidt	433	$10.50
Vol. 3	"Schoolhouse Treasures 3 - Blackbird Inn" by Cathy Schmidt	518	$10.50
Vol. 1	"Holiday Hangarounds" by Marsha Sellers	327	$10.50
Vol. 1	"Huckleberry Friends" by Cheryl Seslar	393	$10.50
Vol. 2	"Huckleberry Friends 2" by Cheryl Seslar	403	$10.50
Vol. 3	"Huckleberry Friends 3" by Cheryl Seslar	431	$10.50
Vol. 1	"Kindred Hearts" by Viki Sherman....*NEW*	532	$10.50
Vol. 1	"Friendship Creek" by Katherine Smith	496	$10.50
Vol. 1	"Creations In Canvas...and More" by Carol Spooner	256	$10.50
Vol. 1	"Gran's Garden" by Ros Stallcup	295	$10.50
Vol. 2	"Another Gran's Garden" by Ros Stallcup	315	$10.50
Vol. 3	"Gran's Garden & House" by Ros Stallcup	334	$10.50
Vol. 4	"Gran's Garden Party" by Ros Stallcup	345	$10.50
Vol. 5	"Gran's Treasures" by Ros Stallcup	363	$10.50
Vol. 6	"Gran's Gifts" by Ros Stallcup	387	$10.50
Vol. 10	"Gran's Magic-Bells, Books & Candles" by Ros Stallcup	466	$12.95
Vol. 11	"Gran's Attic" by Ros Stallcup	483	$12.95
Vol. 12	"Gran's Pantry" by Ros Stallcup	508	$12.95
Vol. 13	"Gran's Cottage" by Ros Stallcup....*NEW*	533	$12.95
Vol. 1	"Storybook Lane - Harber Boy's Collection" by Sandy Starkel	520	$10.50
Vol. 2	"Blackberry Hollow" by Margaret Steed	407	$10.50
Vol. 1	"Keepsakes For The Holidays" by Charleen Stempel & S. Scheewe	286	$10.50
Vol. 1	"Christmas Greetings from the Cottage" by Chris Stokes	336	$10.50
Vol. 1	"Christmas Visions" by Max Terry	278	$10.50
Vol. 3	"Painting Clay Pot-pourri" by Max Terry	310	$10.50
Vol. 3	"Country Primitives 3" by Maxine Thomas	322	$10.50
Vol. 4	"Country Primitives 4" by Maxine Thomas	350	$10.50
Vol. 7	"Country Primitives 7" by Maxine Thomas	459	$10.50
Vol. 8	"Country Primitives 8" by Maxine Thomas	482	$10.50
Vol. 1	"Rise & Shine" by Jolene Thompson	214	$6.50
Vol. 2	"The Garden Gate" by Jolene Thompson	250	$10.50
Vol. 5	"Count Your Blessings" by Chris Thornton	213	$10.50
Vol. 6	"Share Your Blessings" by Chris Thornton	226	$10.50
Vol. 7	"Blessings" by Chris Thornton	255	$10.50
Vol. 9	"Blessings For The Home" by Chris Thornton	275	$10.50
Vol. 11	"Painted Blessings" by Chris Thornton	323	$10.50
Vol. 12	"Family Blessings" by Chris Thornton	349	$10.50
Vol. 15	"Multitude of Blessings" by Chris Thornton	379	$10.50
Vol. 17	"Blessings For The Home & Garden" by Chris Thornton	423	$12.95
Vol. 18	"Blessings To Treasure" by Chris Thornton	438	$10.50
Vol. 19	"Blessings To Share" by Chris Thornton	470	$10.50
Vol. 20	"Blessings In A Jar" by Chris Thornton	494	$10.50
Vol. 21	"Blessings In A Jar 2" by Chris Thornton	505	$10.50
Vol. 22	"Blessings In A Jar 3" by Chris Thornton....*NEW*	546	$10.50
Vol. 2	"Farmer and Friends" by Lou Ann Trice	366	$10.50
Vol. 1	"Jars, Jars, Jars!" by Cindy Trombley	469	$10.50
Vol. 2	"Jars, Jars, Jars! 2" by Cindy Trombley....*NEW*	537	$10.50
Vol. 1	"Bear's Inn Jars" by Paula Walsh....*NEW*	539	$10.50
Vol. 5	"Daydreams & Sweet Shirts II" by Don & Lynn Weed	208	$10.50
Vol. 1	"Pitter-Patter-Pigtail-Girls! A Simpler Thyme"by Stacy Gross West	432	$10.50
Vol. 2	"Country Doodles 2" by Amanda Williams	484	$10.50
Vol. 1	"All Of The Holidays" by Chris Williams	443	$10.50
Vol. 1	"Connie's Favorite Old-Time Labels" by Connie Williams	335	$10.50
Vol. 2	"Connie's Garden Seed Packets" by Connie Williams	351	$10.50
Vol. 1	"Floral Fabrics and Watercolor" by Sally Williams	262	$10.50
Vol. 1	"A Time For Giving" by Evelyn Wright	308	$10.50

VISA MasterCard

SHIPPING & HANDLING CHARGES
Add $3.00 for the First Book for shipping and handling.
Add $1.50 per each additional book.
Please Add $4.00 for handling & postage. PER TAPES.
Sorry we must have a "NO REFUND - NO RETURN" policy.

Check out our WEB SITE at: http://www.painting-books.com   e-mail us at: scheewepub@aol.com